SHOCK
TREATMENTS!

My Struggles with Depression
and Various Treatments for It

Emily Eastman

authorHOUSE®

AuthorHouse™
1663 Liberty Drive
Bloomington, IN 47403
www.authorhouse.com
Phone: 1 (800) 839-8640

Interior Graphics/Art Credit: Lois Pontius

Published by AuthorHouse   09/28/2015

ISBN: 978-1-5049-4927-9 (sc)
ISBN: 978-1-5049-4928-6 (e)

Library of Congress Control Number: 2015914853

Print information available on the last page.

This book is printed on acid-free paper.

Contents

Introduction

The author of this book, Emily Eastman, passed away suddenly of a pulmonary embolism on August 20, 1983, almost three years to the day after her husband, Phil, passed away. She had every intention of getting the book published. She felt she had a message to convey. Her children and grandchildren decided to attempt to carry out her plans to get it published, and they are finally getting around to acting on that decision. It is a true story, and she changed the names and places to protect the privacy of persons in the story. Unfortunately, she did not have the advantage of a computer to write this; she hammered it out on a manual typewriter. She was a woman ahead of her time. She would have loved the computer technology if she had ever had a chance to use it.

Just a word regarding the political correctness of her language. She uses the term "colored" for the people that today we call "African Americans." That was an accepted terminology at that time. She certainly was not a racist. In the fifties, she may have been the only white person who was outraged by the substandard school building that the black students had to attend in town (out by the city dump) while the white students had a nice modern brick building. She taught her children that the use of racial or ethnic slurs was just as objectionable as the use of profanity. She would never have deliberately used a racial slur. Also, her use of the word "crippled" was in common usage then before the invention of the term "physically challenged."

You will notice throughout the book comments in brackets. While she was editing the manuscript and getting it ready for publication, Caroline interjected some comments recalling her memories of what happened at that time or her impression of it.

Chapter 1

Depression

I sat, glued to my chair, afraid to move. It was a spring day in 1957, and I was silently waiting for the thin man sitting just a few feet away from me to speak. He was watching my face so intently. Why doesn't he say something? I squirmed inwardly, wondering what he expected me to do. I had expected him to ask me questions, but he seemed to expect me to talk without being asked. Desperately, I tried to think of something to say, but my mind was a blank. While I imagined he was thinking, "start talking," I felt like screaming at him to "start talking." My anxiety grew, and I wanted to make a dash for freedom. I felt like a criminal waiting for the judge to pass a life or death sentence on me. But he wasn't a judge; he was a doctor and was supposed to help me. Yet, I wanted to get away from him. Just a few minutes before, when I had first sat down in the chair facing this doctor with such dark brown eyes and he had asked me a few routine questions, a feeling had come over me that this doctor would be different from the others and would really do something for me. Gradually, however, my optimism left me. He wasn't even going to try. My fear became mixed with a kind of anger. He was worse than any of the others. He watched me in silence. After having waited in the waiting room in almost stark terror, wondering what the doctor would be like and jumping at every rustle or noise and watching the hall in both directions, I finally saw him come into view around the corner. Coming toward me and putting out his hand to shake hands, he had introduced himself. Like a sheep following the leader to the slaughter I had followed him back around the corner and into this small room with a large Venetian-blind-covered picture window. Mrs. Gray, the social worker from our county had brought me to the Baxter County Health Center about 50 miles from home to see this doctor. At the time, she was in the waiting room, trying to keep my two youngest children quiet. Cynthia, two-and-a-half, and Edward, one year old, had both been born after I was forty. My five older ones were in school.

My mind continued a blank, while Dr. Banks watched me, saying nothing, while fear and anger raged inside me. Suddenly the silence of the room was broken. A tiny voice from the hall began to cry, "Mommy, Mommy, Mommy," as she pounded the door with her tiny fists. Cynthia, having wriggled away from Mrs. Gray, had found the door where I had disappeared, but she was too short to reach the knob. "Mommy. Mommy." She sounded so pathetic. I wanted to go and pick her up, but I was afraid. If I'm quiet, I thought, maybe she'll go away. She didn't and continued to cry in distress. When I didn't answer her, she started to pound on the door with her small fists. I shivered; the doctor watched; Cynthia pounded. "Open the door and let her come inside," the doctor finally said. I felt relieved. Cynthia snuggled her little red head up against me contentedly. The doctor looked at her, and then I was surprised to see him scoot his chair up closer and poke her little freckled nose and say, "She's a cute little devil." I beamed with motherly pride. His apparent interest in Cynthia, however, seemed to be short-lived. He again started watching me and saying nothing. I hugged Cynthia more closely, and my anxiety returned.

I don't really know when my depressions had first begun, but the spells had become much more severe when I was nineteen and a senior in high school. I was second to the oldest in a large family. My parents had ten children, although two had died very young. Amelia, my sister two years older than I, and Carl, my brother two years younger, and I spent most of our elementary school years in a small country school in a sparsely populated area in Montana. In the small school, the other girls had always seemed to be nearer Amelia's age than mine, and I had felt terribly left out and rejected at school. At home, however, I had Amelia. She had been almost like a second mother to all the younger kids, and I know my folks had depended a lot on her. I remembered her as being generous toward the rest of us and overly protective—especially toward me. I thought she knew everything, and I think the younger brothers and sisters did too. She was a bit bossy, perhaps because of the responsibility placed on her and maybe some being a natural talent as an executive. I just naturally did what she told me to do, and yet, there were times when I resented her always giving me the easy jobs and taking the hard ones herself and saying to me, "You can't." Nevertheless, I respected her authority.

Carl, however, was a different story. He loved to fight—that is, wrestle—and I made a good dummy for practicing sessions, so he could whip the other boys at school. So he would say, "Come on, let's have a fight," or torment me until I had to fight for self-preservation. I had to fight for my life or run for it, and lots of times I ran. I studied hard and skipped the fourth grade and caught up with the other kids older than I was and was called "teacher's pet," alienating me more than ever.

Since Amelia had missed a lot of school because of illness and to help at home, we graduated from the eighth grade the same year. Amelia went to the small high school the following year, and I stayed home to herd cows. My folks didn't believe in high school, but a man had come around and coaxed them to send us, and Mama had believed it would be better to send her, since I was younger and might have a chance later. I accepted it as reasonable, although I don't remember ever thinking I might go later.

The next year we moved to Iowa where all our relatives were, and neither of us went to school. The following year, however, I got a chance to stay in town and work for my room and board. My folks let me start, believing I would soon tire of it and quit on my own. I didn't, though, and I mopped floors, washed windows, did washings and ironings and rubbed the neurotic woman's back. I got good grades but had few friends and very little social life. Each year my folks tried to get me to quit, but I refused. In my senior year, I started dating Herb, an older man, and began having spells of depression. I now wanted to quit school, but Mama said, "No, you're not. You've gotten such good grades, you're going to finish."

Consequently, I graduated in the spring of 1933 as valedictorian, when I was 20 and two years older than most of my classmates. Having taken the Normal Teaching course the last two years, I was eligible to teach in one of the many one-room country schools scattered around over the country. I got a school that fall through the recommendation of one of my classmates, who had an uncle who was a director. I was thrilled and at the same time scared to death. I had very little self-confidence in my ability to do anything that might seem a little difficult. Amelia had taken the lead for so long, and I had the "I can't" drilled into me. The school was large, with all grades except the third and with several good-sized boys in it. I tried hard, but at the end of three months, I lost it because of discipline.

I became terribly depressed and dreamed about the school for a month afterwards. I'm a failure, rang through my head, day after day. My family started scolding me for having the blues, and Carl told me I wore my heart on my sleeve, so I tried to hide my disappointment. Three months later, Herb jilted me, saying "I don't want to marry anyone who can't even teach school. You didn't even feel bad. I felt worse than you did." I was hurt and completely baffled. Hate and anger and hopelessness filled me. So, I wasn't even fit to get married because I'd been a failure as a teacher. Failure, failure, failure rang in my ears. My family and relatives gave me pep talks more than ever, which only made me feel more inferior. I wasn't strong like they were.

I just listened to them. At first I tried losing myself by going with boys I cared nothing for and tried having a good time. It didn't work. I was left with an empty feeling, so I tried to bury myself in work. I took jobs scrubbing floors and washing dishes. Domestic jobs were plentiful in spite of the depression of the 1930's. But even these jobs left me feeling inferior. If a job came along taking care of a new-born baby, Mama said to the would-be employer, "Emily can't do that kind of work. Amelia can, but she'll have to have more money." I was a failure and good for nothing. Mama was right, I thought, when she said, "If it had been Amelia teaching, she wouldn't have lost the school." In the spring, I had some dates with Raymond, and when I felt such a strong attraction for him, I tried to stop going with him. I'd only get hurt.

From the first, I'd felt differently about Raymond than I had about Herb. I felt that this time I was really in love. So in spite of my attempts to quit him, I couldn't as long as he came to see me. He was a hard worker and didn't smoke or drink and was well-thought-of by his acquaintances and neighbors, but he was independent and prided himself on the name. In time, he became independent with me. He had me in hot water all the time. I put up with it, feeding his ego to his heart's content. He came when he pleased and broke dates the same way. In the meantime, I'd given up trying to get another school. Then one of Mama's brothers was elected director, and, in spite of there being a sort of rule that they couldn't hire blood relatives, he offered me the school. It wasn't a law, but some people thought it was, and immediately there was a kick. Too many other girls wanted the school. This school was much smaller, with only five grades to teach, and five of the pupils were my cousins. I kept the school the full nine months, but at the end of the term, when my uncle offered me the school again, I told him to forget it. Under the circumstances, I was sure there would be trouble before it was all over.

After I put my application in for several schools with no luck, I finally gave up trying. With so many girls begging for schools, it was almost impossible to get one without a pull. Although I hadn't been fired from my uncle's school, some people seemed to think I had, and I think I began to feel I had. So, with Raymond's treatment of me and keeping me guessing and my feeling of being a failure, my depressions deepened, and my relatives increased their pep talks.

In 1937, Raymond's mother decided to hire me as her "hired girl." She thought no girl was good enough for one of her boys, and now she had me where she wanted me. She could point out all my faults to her boy. I worked all summer for her, while she and one of her other boys gave me a rough time. I was getting more nervous all the time, until I began to realize something was going to have to give. I'd heard of nervous breakdowns and was afraid I was about to have one.

That fall Phil Eastman from Missouri, a cousin of Raymond's, came to Iowa to work in the wheat harvest and then stayed for corn picking. At first, he believed the stories and complaints he heard, and then decided they were just figments of his relatives' imaginations. He started sympathizing with me. When the harvest was over and he went back to Missouri, he asked me to write to him, and I did. My job also ended, and I went home to recuperate from the ordeal I'd been through. I was sure by this time that I was on the verge of a nervous breakdown and fought desperately to ward it off. I had offers of several domestic jobs, but for a couple of weeks couldn't bring myself to take them.

Finally, I did take one and found myself working for one of the worst neurotic women I'd ever worked for. I was still writing to Phil, and he began to ask me to marry him. I told him I still loved Raymond, but, as he continued to insist, the temptation began to take hold of my imagination. What was love, anyway, I asked myself. There really is no such thing. It was something in fairy tales and love stories. I might feel better if I had a home of my own and wouldn't have to work for all these neurotic women who couldn't be pleased.

I finally consented, with my relatives all saying I was doing the right thing; although they knew how I felt about Raymond. We went to live with Phil's folks, since his mother, a diabetic, was on crutches at the time and needed help, but with the understanding we would move to a place of our own in the spring, when his mother's condition would be better.

But when spring came and her leg was no better, I agreed to our staying together for a while longer. My mother-in-law had a happy disposition and had accepted me as part of the family, but her constant chattering and her habit of telling everyone around her almost every move to make began to grate on my nerves. The fact that I needed to be by her side a lot of the time and was expecting a baby didn't help. She was beside herself with joy at the chance to take care of a newborn baby again. She had worked in people's homes when she was a girl and had taken care of babies the same as Amelia had. Her talking about this reminded me about my inferiority again.

When Mark was born, the strain became much greater when Phil's mother was glad to give me all the advice she could on how to raise my baby. She didn't mind it at all, since she knew that I knew nothing about babies, she told me. I felt so helpless. She meant well, I knew, and she wasn't so young anymore. I felt guilty when it irritated me so much. I gritted my teeth and tried to take it in stride. But in August, when Mark was about four months old, I became so tense as she purred contentedly by my side, unaware of my feelings, that I had urges to pick up a chair and throw it at her. I became frightened, thinking I must be going crazy, and told Phil I should go to the doctor. Dr. Jackson gave me some little green pills and some dark brown liquid and recommended the two families separate. "No house is big enough for two women," he said. I wondered, if I had been 16 instead of 26, would things have worked out better?

After Phil's folks moved to a house in town, I still felt tense and guilty. I seemed unable to get the feeling the house was mine. Mark wasn't mine; he was only a brother or a cousin I was baby-sitting with. I still felt angry toward my mother-in-law. I worked hard, raising chickens and a large garden and canning and helping Phil in the field when I could, but my housework got behind. I felt guilty about that.

I had a neighbor woman whose only daughter lived a couple of hundred miles away. She was lonesome and came to see me two or three times a week. She thought she was helping me out, too, since I also lived far from my mother. She was nice, and I knew she meant well when she seemed to step right into Phil's mother's place and gave me advice on how to raise my baby. It didn't help any that he was active and mischievous. I could almost always count on his doing something off-beat whenever she made her call. If she'd tell me I shouldn't let him do this or that (the only time he did it might be when she was there), I imagined I saw a gleam of delight in Mark's eyes. Did he like to irritate the nice lady, or did he like to see me get scolded? If I saw her coming up the walk, I'd get an urge to hide him in a closet or something and actually caught myself looking around for just such a place. I worried about the finances, but Phil was an optimist and seemed content to let me do all the worrying. When Mark was two, Caroline was born, and we then got a Farm Security Loan. I kept the books and worried if they didn't balance to the penny.

When we were married, Phil and I had belonged to different churches, but after a two-week evangelistic meeting in his church, I saw some sense in the basic belief of his church—the whole Bible and nothing but the Bible and only Christ as the head of the church. I was baptized, but when I saw some of the older members teaching the very things they preached against, I became discouraged and confused about religion.

When Caroline was two, we moved to a smaller farm, and Toby was born. After his birth, I seemed unable to gain back my strength and had spells of deep depression. I was able to do my own work and to keep the FSA books perfectly. I worried more than ever and lost weight. I had a chronic pain in my thigh that I called rheumatism and mostly ignored, but others noticed my limping. I began to have obsessive thoughts about hypnotism and losing my school. I was a failure. I started having spells where my fingers and thumbs would stiffen out like boards and turn white. I told Phil about my feelings and wondered if I might have what they called an inferiority complex. So Phil asked Dr. Jackson if there was such a thing as an inferiority complex, and Dr. Jackson said there certainly was and that I seemed to have it pretty bad.

When Toby was nine months old, Phil's mother died. The night before the funeral, I got terribly sick on a can of sardines. I went to the funeral, however, and after the services, my fingers and thumbs started turning white and getting stiff. But this time it spread to my whole arms, and they called a doctor for me—one I'd never seen before. Later, a friend told me that while the doctor was in the kitchen, he said, "It's just her nerves. I can't explain it, but some people just can't stand to go to funerals. She's just weak and nervous."

After that, the friend harped on my being weak and nervous. I knew that the funeral had nothing to do with it, unless, because of my run-down condition, the excitement was too much for me. I was sure the sardines had helped it along, but nobody would listen to me. I worried more and more and wondered why I was so much different from everyone else. What did people mean when they said I was weak and nervous? About a month later, I had a complete collapse and went to bed for a week and couldn't even stand on my feet. Phil called Mama, and she came down and became all excited when Dr. Jackson said I had a psychoneurotic condition. She thought it was a nice name for crazy. Phil seemed unable to get it across to her that that was not the case.

Once Phil had asked Dr. Jackson if there was danger of my becoming psychotic. At first he said there was. Then later he said he didn't think there was, since I had so much insight into my condition. He told Phil that they might help me at the State Hospital, but they wouldn't take me, because I wasn't bad enough.

I went home with Mama and stayed for a month, then came back home, leaving Caroline and Toby with my folks. I took Mark with me, since he was almost on the verge of a nervous breakdown, himself, I thought, and I was afraid my family wouldn't understand him.

That fall, after several reverses, Phil decided to sell off the livestock and go to Iowa and work as a "hired man." By this time, my folks and Amelia had made up their minds that I wasn't capable of doing my own thinking. I couldn't keep my housework up, and they scolded me for that and made me feel more guilty than ever. Chuck, my fourth baby, was born shortly after moving to Iowa. In spite of having less worry about money, I still had my spells of depression. My family worked on me and told me how terrible I was. I was weak and nervous and couldn't stand anything.

Finally, I bought some books to see if I could learn what really was so wrong with me. Some of them helped me understand things somewhat better, but my family still scolded and said it was the books that were making me go crazy. This didn't make sense, since they had been telling me I was crazy before I had ever picked up a book of that kind. Actually, the books fascinated me. I decided psychology was really interesting.

I felt like an outcast from my family. I couldn't sleep and tried to get one of my cousins to understand what my family was doing to me, but she had been listening to the other side and seemed to be against me, too. I started having recurrent dreams in which I would be standing facing a long line of relatives and friends and trying to make them understand. They'd only stare back with accusing and unfeeling eyes. Then I'd see Dr. Jackson approaching from the rear, and I would think, now, I'll have help. But when he walked right past me and lined up with the others, I would start screaming and wake up with an uneasy feeling.

Two of my brothers were in the war in France. One was killed in the Battle of the Bulge, but the other one came back. It seemed everyone was upset, and they were harder than ever on me.

One night in 1946, Phil and I were in one of those self-help grocery stores. A group of chattering women sat on the bench along the front of the store. Phil and I started toward the back of the store. I imagined I heard Amelia's voice among the voices in the front. I turned to try to locate the voice. But it seemed to have disappeared.

But now the voice seemed to dwindle down to the level of the other voices. I turned again to the back, and the voice returned. It seemed to stand out louder than any of the others. Yet, I couldn't make out the words. I looked again toward the row of women, and the voice stopped or became mingled with the babble. By this time, I realized it was all in my head. There was no voice, but when we reached the far end of the store, the voice was as loud as it was in the front. I still couldn't make out the words, but all the inflections and tone were there, and it stood out way above the babble.

Depressions and obsessions and worries were one thing, but hearing voices that weren't there was another. It was plainly auditory hallucinations. Phil took me to our family physician, and he sent me to a clinic in a city about 50 miles away.

After asking a few questions, the psychiatrist who gave me the initial examination suddenly jumped from his chair and rushed to where I sat on the examining table, yelling questions as he came and, without giving me a chance, answering them himself with sarcasm. I was stunned as he put the stethoscope to my chest and grasped my wrist, still asking the questions in apparent anger. I was flabbergasted.

Phil, who had come in with me, finally got his speech back and said, "I think you're misunderstanding her, Doctor,"

"I understand," the doctor said in such a kind voice that I could hardly believe my ears. But the damage was done, and after that I clammed up. He sent me home that day with several prescriptions and an order to come back in a month. I wasn't wild about it, but when the month was up, I returned to the clinic. This time, however, a younger psychiatrist saw me. He sat and talked in a kind voice and listened respectfully, and soon I gained some confidence in him. The rest of the summer, I went to see him once a month. He let me talk and occasionally would offer a suggestion. Once he said, "Why don't you try to please yourself once in awhile, instead of the other person?" I was always talking about my housework, since it seemed that was what bothered my family so much. He said, "Stop worrying about your dishes. Don't do them."

This stumped me and I asked, "But how will they get washed?"

"They'll get done," he said, unrealistically, I thought.

I told Mama what he said and she snapped, "He's the one who's crazy; he needs his head examined."

That fall, after I had been going to the psychiatrist about six months, Phil decided to go back to the farm in Missouri. My folks went up in the air about this and tried to stop him, but when they saw he was determined, they tried to keep me from going. I refused. In fact, I was afraid I would go crazy if I stayed with them. Then they were going to make us leave the children with them. I wasn't fit to be a mother.

When we went back to see the doctor for the last time and told him what we were planning, Phil asked, "How bad is she, really?"

"She's not so bad," the doctor said, "because if she were, she couldn't go on month after month the way she has."

"Should we take the children with us?" Phil asked. "Her folks want us to leave them here."

"Take them with you. Children should be with their parents," the doctor replied.

"Should we stop seeing a psychiatrist when we get back to Missouri?" Phil asked.

"No," the psychiatrist answered, "you can find one down there. There are plenty of us around."

We left Iowa, much against my family's wishes. A big fight had taken place, and we parted in great anger. When we got to Missouri, it seemed unbearable to be so on the outs with my family. Yet, I knew I couldn't let them run my life. My emotions were in a constant turmoil. I was an outcast. I was sure my parents weren't enjoying the situation any better than I was, but what could I do? Why wouldn't they understand? My biggest failing had been my inability to keep my house clean, and they made it worse. They had come down and helped me a few times with my work, but after they left, I was in such a state, I couldn't sleep for several days. They had also loaned us some money, which, no doubt, left me feeling more beholden to them than ever.

We went back to the farm, but we now had no machinery or horses, and 80 acres wasn't enough in this day and age to make a living for a family; so Phil tried a garbage route, but it didn't pan out. All he could do now was to take odd jobs wherever he could find them. That spring, when Chuck was two and a half, Henry was born.

That summer, Phil was high-pressured into trying to sell J. B. Watkins products door to door. It turned out worse than the garbage business had. We almost lost our farm and everything we had.

After coming back to Missouri, I had not gone to see a psychiatrist. But that fall, I became so tense and worried because of our financial situation and because of the continuing feud with my family, that Dr. Jackson finally sent me to Dr. Brown in River City, about 50 miles away. Dr. Brown wasn't exactly a psychiatrist, but he had worked at the River City State Hospital, and Dr. Jackson thought he would be good.

I went to see him once a week for four months. After the initial interview, all he did was let me wait in his waiting room for three hours and then have his nurse give me a shot and send me home with several prescriptions without my even seeing him. We began to get discouraged. Why couldn't Dr. Jackson give me the shot? We could, at least, save the gas to make that long trip. We were having enough trouble finding grocery money. That, in itself, was causing me so much worry that I was getting worse instead of better.

Dr. Jackson agreed, if we would find out what the shot was. So the next time, after the nurse had given me my shot, we asked her to let us talk to the doctor. She went out, and he came in and stood over me with what I felt was a plastered-on smile and asked me how I was and was gone. I had no time to ask him anything. When we told Dr. Jackson our experience, he agreed to contact Dr. Brown himself. He fared little better than we had, except to have Dr. Brown tell him I needed shock treatments. I was shocked, all right. What could I do? I was crazy after all; my family was right.

Then circumstances saved me. While Phil was still struggling to try to sell vanilla and pepper and Watkins Cure-all liniment, and going deeper and deeper in debt, our car broke down, and our money gave out. We couldn't go back to see Dr. Brown, if that was what we wanted to do. I could, at least, now forget about that problem.

After that, Phil took jobs around the neighborhood, which didn't pay very much. Besides our living, we had payments on the farm, and his wages didn't cover that. So the following fall, when Henry was one-and-a-half and my oldest was nine-and-a-half, Phil went to River City and got job in a packing plant. I was left with the livestock and the five kids on the farm, while Phil only came home weekends to lay in a supply of groceries and fuel.

That first winter, I had my hands full just sending the two kids to school and caring for the other three and building fires and milking the few cows we had. The next spring, the packing plant began laying him off, and he went to the stockyards and got a job there feeding western lambs. Some of these yearlings dropped lambs, and Phil would come home two or three times a week lugging an armful of the woolly animals for me to raise on the bottle. A neighbor plowed my garden, and I raised chickens. We rented the farming ground out. Phil's working in River City was supposed to have been temporary until we could get on our feet, but there never seemed to come a time when we felt he could afford to give up his weekly check.

I continued to stay on the farm and finally got a team of horses and some colts and learned to plow my own garden with a walking plow. We quit renting our ground, and I mowed and raked hay and plowed corn and built fence and, with Phil's help, even broke colts. With this responsibility and less worry about money, I felt a lot better. Still, I had spells of discouragement and depressions. I'd have spells in which I would just stand and scream. Finally, it dawned on me that these screaming spells came on me at the end of a day when I'd had a housecleaning spree. After this, when I'd start to clean house and felt a tension building up, I would become frightened and would stop, and the screams would be headed off.

Phil continued to work in the city. Toby started school and so did Chuck. When Henry was almost six, and I was almost forty, I had another little girl. I had been looking forward to having her, thinking that, at last, I could enjoy caring for my baby without having someone to tell me how. I was disappointed; she only lived a day.

All spring and summer, my emotions were in a turmoil. I wanted another baby and thought I was too old to have one, and, besides, it was silly. If I didn't already have several, it might be different. I felt guilty. I couldn't even do my field work. I'd put the harness on the horses in the morning and let them stand all day and pull it off their backs without ever hitching them to an implement. Dr. Jackson said, his eyes twinkling, "At least you know you still remember how to harness a horse."

My depression got no better, but it seemed to have a pattern. I would get lower and lower and finally go to bed until my mind become a blank, and I'd get up and make a grainy concoction I called fudge. I'd eat it and feel better until the next time. Was it the concoction that helped me or just the act of doing something?

Henry started school that fall. I now had all five kids in school. They were in grades one through eight in the one-room country school. Being alone, I could sit on a disc or plow all day long, and I began to feel better.

As the farms grew larger and rural populations smaller, the country schools were becoming smaller. Many of them had already been consolidated into the town schools. With a total student body of eleven that year, we weren't going to get to keep ours much longer. Mark graduated at the end of that year, along with the two boys who had been his classmates all through the eight years together. He started high school in town that fall and rode the school bus to town. The next year, four of the eight students were mine, and Caroline graduated with the two girls who had been her classmates all through the eight years. That was the end of our little school. We had fought to keep it, but the townspeople outvoted us, and the school was consolidated into the town school. An interesting sidelight is that while my kids were in high school, most of the honor roll students were ones who had come in from the rural grade schools. They seemed to have learned more in eight months in the country schools than the town kids had in nine months each school year. Actually, it was largely a matter of attitude. The country kids were so naïve as to think that the main purpose for going to school was to learn something. They had the notion that they and the parents and the teacher had a common goal, while the town kids took somewhat of an adversarial position toward the teacher.

Now all five of the older kids had to meet the school bus. I'd be so nervous after getting them off so as not to miss it that when they were gone, I'd sit down and drink one cup of coffee after another, no doubt making me more nervous than ever. I began to feel better, however, and my relationship with my family had greatly improved. Still, I felt on the outside at times.

In November of the last year of our country school, a year and a half after I'd lost my baby, when I was forty-one, Cynthia was born. A year and a half later, when I was forty-three, Edward was born on Phil's 47th birthday. I still felt insecure and like a nit-wit who knew nothing about babies. Every so often I'd go into a deep depression. I had no social life—or very little—and would feel that Phil was pushing too much of the responsibilities onto me. We'd have our differences.

One day, in a fit of despondency and feeling I wasn't giving the kids the care they should have and with the older ones in school, I hitch-hiked to town about five miles away and into the Welfare Office and said, "Here, take my babies and take care of them; I can't."

Mrs. Gray took charge of me, and, after talking to me, she took me home and began to make trips to my home at intervals, until the Welfare Board put a stop to it, saying we weren't indigent and, therefore, I wasn't eligible. She continued to try to find one thing and another where I might go for help, but always there seemed to be some reason I wasn't entitled to the service, and we were too poor to go to a private psychiatrist.

Now, she'd found this, a service paid for by the State of Missouri. She called it the Traveling Clinic. She could take me the first time, she said, but after that, I'd have to find some other transportation.

So here I sat, facing this strange doctor who didn't talk. I hoped he could help me but was afraid he couldn't. "Wouldn't" might be a better word, I thought, as my anxiety grew and I got madder and madder at him. "Come back in two weeks," he finally said. "I want my psychologist to give you some psychological tests." I left the room, not knowing what to think, but at least he was going to do something none of the others had bothered to do. He was going to give me some kind of tests.

Chapter 2

Shock Treatments

Two weeks went by. It was time to go back and take those tests. Phil had bought me an old black Chevy so I could drive and he wouldn't have to miss work to take me. School was out now, so the older kids could watch the two small ones while I took them. It scared me to drive that far away from home without Phil, but I made it.

The psychologist who gave me the tests was nice, but her high heels clicking on the floor bothered me. I never liked to wear them myself and wondered why any woman would, especially when they were working. They looked so uncomfortable.

I worked on the tests for an hour or more in the morning. They gave me an hour off at noon for lunch, and I went to the car and found a bunch of tired and hungry kids, so I took them for a ride, and we went over the hill about a mile away to the shopping center and got something to eat. The Health Center seemed to be in the country with farming ground all around it, but the county seat was just over the hill and out of sight.

At one, I went back and finished the tests. After I finished, I sat down in the waiting room to wait for the doctor to talk to me. I felt weak and shaky, and then I saw the doctor standing at the information desk a few feet away talking to the psychologist. I was stunned when I heard her say, "It's a mess. It's all mixed up; maybe you can make something out of it; I can't." I was scared now. Were they talking about me? Was I all mixed up. I was depressed, but surely not that bad.

I'd been staying on the farm alone with the kids. If I was that bad, I surely couldn't have done that. I could do my work, except that the housework got terribly behind, but then I did other work to make up for it. I recognized reality, even when I went to bed and my head felt all stuffed with cotton. I must have been fairly normal. But maybe he was talking about someone else. It wasn't me that was all mixed up.

Why did he keep doing that? Why did he look at me and not say anything? He seemed so calm and unhurried, even though he did seem interested. What was he thinking? Then I heard him say something about a hospital in a quiet voice. Ready to grasp at anything, I blurted out, "We have Blue Cross."

He studied my face intently for a few seconds and then said, "You need shock treatments." I was stunned and frightened and tried to protest, but he only watched me in silence and then said, "It won't cost you anything. The Blue Cross will pay the hospital, and although my fee is usually larger, I'll do it for the Blue Cross."

I still protested; there was more than the money holding me back. I didn't want any part of shock treatments. They'd only turn me into a robot. It was bad enough to get shocked on my electric fence when I opened the gate to let the cows come through it. I was afraid of electricity.

He took his time to answer again, and I almost thought I'd changed his mind. Then I saw him pick up the phone and ring the girl at the information desk. I knew I hadn't. "Who is your family physician?" he asked. I told him. He asked if he was on the same exchange as we were. Dr. Jackson was on a different exchange than ours, and there was nothing to do but tell him the truth. Dr. Banks asked me for the number, but I didn't have that in my head. "Information can give us that, anyway," he said, still appearing to be calm but interested. He gave the girl all the information and hung up the receiver to wait for her to call back when she got Dr. Jackson. He turned to me and tried to reassure me some more, telling me it would only be nine treatments, and I'd only have to be hospitalized three weeks. I would take three treatments a week, and then I could go home. I still felt helpless and shook my head in protest, hoping, unrealistically, that Dr. Jackson would be out of his office. It would be very unlikely, since he made his home calls in the morning and was in his office in the afternoon.

I squirmed in misery when the girl had Dr. Jackson on the line and Dr. Banks started to talk. He told Dr. Jackson who he was and explained that he had me in the room with him. "She needs shock treatments, and she needs them badly," he told Dr. Jackson. He went on to explain why I needed them, and now I felt hurt as well as scared. He described me in such unflattering terms, as though I was unable to understand. Anger seeped through my fear. He was ignoring me, as if I were a baby and couldn't understand his words—as if I were an article instead of a human being. Riding on a disc all day long with the wind blowing on my face and through my hair and filling it with dust wasn't conducive to good grooming. Milking cows and digging in the garden didn't help my fingernails. Pumping water with a hand pump and carrying it into the house and heating it on the stove and taking a bath in a round galvanized wash tub and never going any place was no encouragement either. What did he know about all this? "She could," the doctor was saying, "but if she did, she'd have to stay there three months. In a private hospital, she would only have to stay three weeks while I give her the treatments, and then she would be released." The State Hospital. That's what they were talking about. I hadn't thought of that. Fear hit me again. The walls were building up around me.

"It won't cost her a thing. The Blue Cross will pay the hospital. I'll do it for what it pays." So Dr. Jackson had told him we couldn't afford a private hospital. But nothing was going to turn Dr. Banks' head. He'd made up his mind. I wondered what he expected Dr. Jackson to do about it and decided Dr. Jackson must have asked him that very thing when he said, "She's reluctant to take them; it's up to you to convince her."

After returning the receiver to the hook, he turned to me and said, "When you're ready to take them, call me and let me know, and I'll reserve a bed for you in one of the hospitals. I'm not sure which one it will be."

That was it. It sounded so final. Shock treatments or nothing. What could I do? So that weekend, Phil and I went to see Dr. Jackson. Although Phil was against them the same as I was, Dr. Jackson, I learned, was on the psychiatrist's side. He told me, "You've wanted help for so long. Now you have the chance; take it."

I did my best to make him see that shock treatments weren't the answer. In the end, however, I decided to take them, but first I'd have to get some things squared away. Someone would have to care for the livestock, and someone would have to care for the kids. We finally decided that Chuck and Edward would go to Phil's sister's, and Caroline and Cynthia would go to my folks. Toby had his job on the dairy farm, and Henry and Mark would stay on the farm and care for the livestock.

We made the arrangements with Dr. Banks, and then I started to worry. The more I thought about it, the more I was sure I could never go through with it. The kids were all parceled out among relatives, and I was all ready to go to the hospital. I simply couldn't. So the day before I was to go, I went to see Dr. Jackson. I told him I couldn't. I had changed my mind. He insisted I go. Later someone told me I became so agitated that I started to fight him. He calmed me down, and in the end I gave up. I would go.

It was early Monday morning the last of June in 1957 when Phil drove me to the large city where Dr. Banks had his office and parked the car on a quiet one-way street in front of a four-storey building. There was nothing forbidding about the simple design of the brick structure and the well-kept lawn on either side of the walk. But once inside, a creepy feeling came over me. The place seemed deserted. We looked around the room with high ceilings and huge open doorways. To me, a spooky glow invaded the place. With cobwebs and draped furniture, it could have been a haunted house. Not a soul was present except us. The information desk in one corner was empty. This was no hospital, I thought.

"Let's get out of here," I whispered to Phil. "We're in the wrong place. This is no hospital."

"This is it," he assured me, seeming sure of himself.

"It can't be," I said. I was on edge, half expecting someone to come and run us out because we were trespassing on private property. What was wrong with Phil, I wondered. Couldn't he feel it? This eerie atmosphere couldn't possibly be a hospital. He ignored me while I tried to peer around corners and into rooms without disturbing the ghosts until, finally, a real live girl did appear. She took down the usual information and our Blue Cross number and then asked for a down payment, which surprised us, since previously hospitals had always admitted us with only the Blue Cross number. She let it go, however, when Phil agreed to transfer our other insurance to be paid directly to them instead of to us. We were then taken to a small room, where a thin wiry little woman doctor with a strong foreign accent interviewed us. Before she had finished, someone came and said to me, "Bring your suitcase and come with me; I want to show you your room."

We went upstairs to the second floor, where she showed me to a small room with two cots in it and a chest of drawers and introduced me to the lady who was already there. The attendant left, and immediately the other lady, very friendly, started talking. She asked me which cot I wanted and which drawers in the chest I would like to have. I didn't care; all I wanted to do was get back to Phil, who must still be talking to the doctor. Would he come to me before he left for work? The lady was telling me how there was nothing wrong with her; she just got tired every so often and came there for a rest. Was she a millionaire, I wondered, a VIP trying to hide away from her adoring public?

Then she left, and I was left all alone, huddling on the cot in fear, almost afraid even to turn my head. I heard a noise in the hall. It got louder and louder and sounded like a bunch of teenagers just let out of school. I heard laughing and joking and a general hullaballoo. Soon, a couple of women came, and they left through the door taking the laughing crowd with them. The noise stopped, and I wondered where they'd gone, but my fear overshadowed my curiosity. I was alone. Everything seemed so quiet. I was beginning to think I wouldn't see Phil before he had to leave for River City to go to work. They had no intention of bringing him to me, nor were they going to take me to him. I was still sitting on my cot, afraid to move, when another woman came and told me to bring my luggage; she was moving me to another room.

I followed her down the long hallway and into a much larger room with three cots in it instead of two. It also had a large dressing table along one side with a large mirror over it and wardrobes on either side. I was scared. What did this mean?

The rest of that first day is a blank in my memory. I knew I wasn't supposed to take a treatment until Wednesday. Instead, I was going to take some sort of tests—electrocardiogram, perhaps, and others. I can't remember taking them. I do remember later, however, when the others returned to their rooms. I was reticent to leave my room, even though I saw others come and go from one room to another. I'd peek out the door and look down the long hall. I saw a room across the hall and finally got up enough nerve to go out in the hall and look in it. There were no cots there—only easy chairs and a television set. Others went in.

I began to wonder what was going on when all the others started to congregate in the hall. I noticed that when a name was called, someone would go and pick up a tray. My tray had been brought to me in my room at noon, and I had supposed it would be again. I waited. Soon I heard a name called. It was my maiden name, and, without thinking, I stepped forward and then felt silly when I saw a black-haired woman pick it up. When mine was called, I took my tray and went to my room and ate alone.

After supper, I saw doctors come to see their patients and felt lonesome. Where was my doctor? I waited for Phil to come. Nobody came, and I wandered around aimlessly. Finally a young woman came to me and asked me to play pool with her. I was surprised. I'd never thought of women playing pool. Anyway, where was there a pool table? Hazel, who I learned was a nurse and was also one of Dr. Banks' patients, found one. It and a table tennis were in another large room. We hit the balls and then went over to the table tennis, but my heart wasn't in it. I couldn't forget where I was. Nine o'clock came, and a tray of cookies and milk were brought to the TV room, and everyone helped themselves. We went to our rooms to go to bed.

One of my roommates was a young farmer's wife, who had two small boys. She seemed nice. The other woman was older, and she said she had never had any children. I learned she was a business woman, and she said she was going through the menopause. She talked and smoked way up into the night. I noticed the young woman getting impatient with her, as she tried to get her to stop smoking. The young woman didn't smoke and neither did I, but their beds were closer together.

I didn't sleep very well that first night. The shock treatments were on my mind. In the morning, I was the first one to awaken. I lay still, afraid to move. What time should I get up. I better not wake anyone else up. Mrs. Farmer's Wife woke up first and got up and made her bed and read her Bible. I made mine, but I didn't have any Bible to read. Mrs. Business Woman didn't get up until it was almost time for breakfast call, and she didn't make her bed. An employee came in later and made her bed. Which one was right, I wondered. If they had someone to make the beds, maybe we weren't supposed to make them. I again started forward when my maiden name was called, and then stepped back embarrassed. The woman with the name, I learned, was a Cuban.

With breakfast over, I started walking around in circles, and I went into the TV room and sat down. It was on with no one else in the room watching it. We had no television, yet, and I knew nothing about the programs. I didn't know anything about turning the knobs, anyway, and just left it where it was. I was unable to get interested in the shows. My mind was all on shock treatments and wishing that Phil would come.

I'd get up and stand in the hallway and look toward the other end, where I knew the stairway and elevator were. Once, while standing and gazing with a sinking feeling in my stomach, I saw a man step into the hall, as if coming right out of the wall. It seemed he'd materialized from nowhere. A sudden fear gripped me, and the name "Sherlock Holmes" flashed through my mind. I turned, almost in terror, and fled to my room and sat down on my cot. Instantly, I had known who the man was. It was my doctor. I'd felt a desire to talk to him, and now I was scared. I sat, huddled on my cot clasping my hands and shivering. In a moment, he was standing before me and then sat down beside me on the cot. I squeezed my hands tighter.

Quietly and almost timidly, I thought, he reached over and turned over both hands and inspected each fingernail and then criticized the broken ragged nails and told me to manicure them. I felt guilty and then a sudden feeling of attraction for the man came over me, making me feel more guilty than ever. How silly, I thought. I could barely answer him in monosyllabic words. He left with orders to put on makeup besides taking care of my hands. When he'd gone, I felt lifeless and washed-out.

Again, I started wandering around aimlessly from one room to another. Then Hazel came and asked me to play games with her. We went to the room with the table tennis and pool table in it. I played, but my heart wasn't in it. I had shock treatments on my mind.

Later, the two women came and took us to the first floor and outside and down a walk to a new-looking one-storey brick building with a high unpainted board around the back. We went inside the building, where I saw several dining tables on one side and cots and easy chairs and racks with magazines on them on the other side of the room. It was air-conditioned and seemed so cold in there. One of the women had long dark hair put up in a bun on the back of her head. The other woman, Miss Daly, had lighter hair, either gray or bleached or just plain light. She wore lots of make-up and only one earring. I wondered if she'd lost the other one. She was very nice and got a lot of stuff and went to one of the tables the furthermost from the door and got out dolls and pipe cleaners and other things. Marguerite, a little 17-year-old Mexican girl, went with her and started to dress one of the dolls. I went, too, and learned we had to pay for the dolls, but they only cost 75 cents, so I got one and, feeling sentimental, I picked a red-haired one because of Cynthia's red hair. She was the only red-haired one of my children, evidently having inherited it from Phil's mother. Still, being sentimental was unusual for me.

About noon, Marguerite went to the partitioned-off corner and asked for the silverware and began to place them around the tables. No one else seemed the least bit interested, but I helped her. I was sure we didn't have to do it, but the teen-aged girl was on the go constantly. She was a nice little girl. When the steaming hot food arrived, we got our plates filled and found a place at a table. I liked the food, although others complained.

I still felt lost and miserable, although Hazel kept after me to go to the yard to play shuffleboard or catch. Some seemed more sophisticated and played cards, but one woman just lay around all day on a cot. Marguerite liked to play shuffleboard and so did Mrs. White, a woman evidently going through the menopause, who had 13 children. There were times when Mrs. White acted like a giggly school girl. We returned to the main building, where I felt more lost and homesick than ever. I played pool with Hazel, if our technique could have been called that. One of the two men on the floor came and gave us a lesson, while I watched (with mouth wide open) the little balls go in the holes like a bunch of well-trained circus animals. He was a barber, but I thought he must have played pool all the time to be that good. He surely was a professional, I thought.

At supper time, the crowd congregated in the hall, and, again, I started forward when my maiden name was called. I felt self-conscious. The name was a Swede name and seemed out of place for the black-haired Cuban with the Spanish accent. She and Marguerite carried on conversations in Spanish.

Phil came to see me, and then it was snack time and afterwards time to go to bed. Mrs. Business Woman, again, talked and talked and smoked one cigarette after another. The younger woman tried her best to stop her without getting nasty, and I saw her patience wearing thin. I hoped they wouldn't get into a fight.

I slept that night in fits again. The time was getting closer. In the morning I woke up feeling more insecure, wondering if I should make my bed as Mrs. Farmer's Wife did or let the cleaning woman do it the way the other woman did.

At breakfast call, when my name wasn't called, I knew what it meant. Now, all I could do was to stay in my room and shiver. It was no use to hope the doctor might forget me. The crowd left and I was alone. I saw nobody. When I heard a voice ring out loud and clear, "Eastman, to the bathroom," I wanted to run away— anyplace. But I was locked in. I knew I was, because I'd seen the women unlock doors when they took us to the recreation building. I went in fear. Once there, I stayed and stayed, until the voice again called me. I still stayed, and the voice came again, this time sounding much more cranky. I continued to dally, until the voice that demanded my appearance seemed to mean business.

Almost paralyzed with fear, I followed her down the hall. In a daze, I got on the elevator, and we rode to the fourth floor. We went into a room with modern light-colored furniture in it. I sat in a corner chair, and the attendant sat in another chair and didn't talk to me, except to make sure I had all bobby pins and such out of my hair. I remembered having read somewhere, or heard it, that when a criminal was being executed in the electric chair, anything made of metal was removed from the body to keep from making burn marks on it. The attendant said nothing. Everything seemed so quiet and solemn; we could have been in a funeral parlor. I could see a closed door across the hall. Was my doctor behind that door? I waited and waited; it seemed like ages. Then I saw the door open, and my heart gave a leap. Was this it? Only a cart with a sheet-covered body on it was pushed out. It seemed so weird. Cold terror seemed to tie my muscles in knots. Finally the door opened again, and Dr. Banks, without looking in my direction, picked up the telephone and talked and then returned to the room. Sherlock Holmes rushed over me. I shivered.

When I was finally in the room across the hall and sitting on a table or something, with the doctor in front of me, I felt weak and helpless. Slightly aware of some kind of box by the bedside but unwilling to look at it, I thought, this is it. I'm done for. I'll never be the same again. I'll be a robot. The doctor, for the first time, seemed like a doctor, as he spoke pleasantly and pulled my house slippers off my feet and stuck them someplace under the mattress, or whatever I was sitting on. He jabbed a needle in my arm and had me lie down. I felt something being placed on my head, and suddenly I passed out like a flash. The next thing I knew, I was in a large room, trying to wake up. I felt so funny—as if I was nobody and nameless. Yet, I felt unworried. I tried to figure out where I was and who I was. Was I in a morgue? Wherever it was, it wasn't uncomfortable. I tried to sit up but couldn't; I was strapped to the bed with wide harness-like straps. So I lay back down to study. Then a woman in white came and loosened the straps and told me to take my time sitting up. I felt in no hurry, anyway. Just who was I? "Don't try to stand on your feet for a little while," the woman said.

I was in no hurry, so I sat, still trying to make up my mind what it was all about. Gradually, it began to come back to me, and the woman came and took me by the arm when she saw me standing on my feet. I was again taken to the second floor and to my room, the attendant keeping hold of my arm. "Ask for an aspirin if you get a headache," I remembered someone saying. The headache came and I got my aspirin. I ate my lunch alone on the ward and was taken to the recreation room afterwards. Phil came to see me; we had our usual snack before bedtime; Mrs. Business Woman still talked and smoked. I could feel the tension building up between my two roommates. I felt tense. Suppose they get so mad at each other and have a fight. How could I prevent it? I tried to get along with both women. I wasn't happy about the smoking and talking long after we should be asleep, but I would put up with it, no matter what. A fight, even if I was not involved, scared me. The next morning, the younger woman said, "I try to get along with everyone, but I can take just so much. I'm not going to put up with it; I'll tell her off." I could see why it might bother her so much. She was nice, but she seemed to be a slave to routine, I thought. With a set regularity, she read her Bible and went to bed and got up. She seemed to have a time for everything, which was all right, I guessed, but my life had never been built around such a schedule. Working as a domestic had left me changing my way of doing things at the whims of others. I had to adjust to my bosses—many of them neurotics.

I didn't think too much about it when the little Mexican girl started coming to me worrying about her jewelry that she claimed the hospital had taken away from her. I told her they took everything of value away from us for safekeeping. They'd give it back to her when she left. She didn't seem to be satisfied. I told her they'd taken ten dollars away from me, but I wasn't worried about it. She still worried. But then, I thought, my ten dollars was only a drop in the bucket in comparison to the value of her jewelry. This had me puzzled. What would a 17-year-old girl be doing with that much jewelry? Was she only imagining it all? I mentioned this to a woman who was a secretary on the outside and who seemed unable to understand my fear of shock treatments. "No, she's not imagining it; she had everything she says she had," the woman, who seemed very sophisticated, said, and I almost got the feeling by the tone of her voice that the girl had a reason to worry about it. Hazel couldn't understand my fear of shock treatments, either. She wanted Dr. Banks to give her some, she told me, and get it over with fast, but he refused, saying she didn't need them. She was very active and was constantly after me to play something with her. She was also sold on Dr. Banks, constantly telling me what a wonderful doctor he was. She's in love with the doctor, I surmised, a common occurrence with patients toward their psychiatrist. Did she single me out to get me to play with her, I wondered, because she had a sisterly feeling toward me by our having the same doctor, or was it that I was one who would play with her? Marguerite, also, seemed to have me singled out to listen to her worry. She had an obsession about her jewels, and every time I turned around she was at my side. I thought how awful to be so young and have to go through those shock treatments; it was bad enough for us older ones. I mentioned this to the secretary, and she said, "She's lucky to get straightened out while she's young."

I still couldn't see it that way. She was about the same age as Caroline; the thought gave me cold chills. Besides, I understand she was taking both electric shock and insulin shock. I only got ECT (electroconvulsive therapy), and some told me I was lucky. Insulin was much worse, they said. I felt unlucky to be getting anything at all, but I was glad I wasn't getting the other. Besides playing shuffleboard and catch in the yard, Marguerite was after me to play Chinese checkers with her, and Herman, the other man on the ward, wasn't satisfied until he got me to play the regular checkers with him. He'd beaten everyone else and was champion. I played and beat him, and then I felt bad about it. It seemed to mean so much to him. I didn't try very hard after that. Shock treatments were my big worry. I still felt listless and disinterested in things around me and wanted to get away from it all. I watched the hall anxiously, hoping to see Phil or my doctor. But when I again saw Dr. Banks step off the elevator as if materializing from out of the wall, the name Sherlock Holmes flashed through my mind, and I dashed to my room and sat down. While I cowered, as if waiting for the bomb to explode, the doctor again sat down beside me and again quietly turned my hands over and again told me to file my nails and put red polish on them. I had put natural polish on when I was a girl at times but never red. The same unexplainable attraction came over me. It didn't make sense. He must have been ten years younger than I was. I felt guilty.

Finally, my younger roommate did tell the older woman off, but it did no good. Mrs. Business Woman took it good-naturedly and went on talking and smoking. I did notice, however, that her bed was moved closer to my bed, so our heads were only a couple feet apart. Either the employees saw the friction, or the young woman complained.

Friday I took my second shock treatment, and I felt more scared than ever, although I knew, now, there was no pain to them except for the headache afterwards. I tarried in the bathroom as long as I dared, but I came out in the end. There was no treatment on Saturday, but the doctor came to see me, and the same mixture of fear and attraction and guilt came over me. Phil came to see me on Sunday, bringing Mark and Henry with him. I was determined to go out for the day, but the hospital refused, because the doctor hadn't left any such order. The boys went, however, since they'd come with the intention of going to a show. I was terribly disappointed, but Phil, I thought, had a good time visiting with the other patients and their relatives. He always got acquainted so much more easily than I did. When my doctor came later, I made sure to ask him to leave an order so I could leave the hospital the next Sunday. The following week, I took my three treatments on Monday, Wednesday and Friday, and on the other days Dr. Banks came to see me. Each time when I'd first see him coming, thoughts of the famous detective would rush over me. At the same time, my attraction for the doctor, or maybe it was just a dependence, as though my life was in his hands, was growing stronger. The magnetic force drawing me to the doctor and my identifying him with Sherlock Holmes and my fear and hatred for the treatments were all scrambled up together. After taking several treatments, I felt less and less confused when waking up and seemed to know who and where I was. Yet, I felt more fear each time. The next Sunday when Phil and the boys came, I was ready for them. I had permission to go out for the day, but now the boys were disappointed. They had seen the pool table and table tennis and the shuffleboard. They had thought it over and had decided this was a fun place and wanted to stay. I won, however, and we went to the zoo. (Later, Phil told me that I was so weak and could barely keep up with them. In fact, sometime later, I had completely forgotten having even gone to the zoo that day, until he had to bring it back to me.)

When Mrs. White began to get giddier and giddier, causing the rest to wonder about it, an attendant explained that she was in shock as a result of the treatments. Mrs. Business Woman still talked at night and lay around all day, even though the nurses got cranky with her. She told me she and her husband had been so busy making money, and they had plenty of it, and then suddenly she just lost interest in everything. Marguerite worried about her jewels, until they gave her a piece or two, but she still worried. The boys didn't come with Phil on the third Sunday, and he didn't take me out, since I would be going home the next day after taking my last ECT. Anxiously, that last morning, with thoughts of going home in my head, I sat on the table ready to take my last—the ninth—treatment. The doctor gave me my shot in the vein, and I lay down. I felt the gear being placed on my head and my temples being greased and something being stuffed in my mouth. Then, just a second before I flashed out, I heard one of the women say in a startled voice, "Oh, my!" When I awakened, I remembered her saying that and wondered why. Had something gone wrong? But I was going home, so this would be the last time. I expected to go home just as soon as I got downstairs, but for some reason, they told me I'd have to wait awhile. I was sure Phil was already there, and I was unable to understand why I had to wait. Nevertheless, the time came, and I walked outside, never, I thought, ever to take another one of those things.

On the road home, Phil told me that the little foreign doctor had asked him that first morning if what I had told her was the truth, and he told her it was pretty much that way. So that was the reason, I thought, for them to take me away before they were finished with Phil. It was also the reason for their putting me in one room and then changing me. If Phil had said something else, I would have been put on the third floor, where the sicker patients were.

So, I thought, my first roommate, who'd said there was nothing wrong with her, hadn't been a patient, after all. She'd been a plant and had really been an employee of the hospital. That was the reason I'd seen her come and go, and she had seldom been at the recreation room with us. She hadn't needed to have the doors unlocked the way they had been for the rest of us. Then Phil told me that he had told Dr. Banks that my family had seemed to think they had to do my thinking for me, and he'd said, "She doesn't need anyone to do her thinking for her. She has enough brains of her own; she can do her own thinking." But when Phil told me the doctor had said that these nine treatments would be enough for now, but I might have to take some more later, I gritted my teeth and said with determination, "No! I'll never take another one." As we rode along on the way home, I felt puzzled by a funny homesick feeling that came over me, as if I hated to leave the hospital. I'd been so anxious to go home, and now I almost felt as if I wanted to return. For three weeks, I'd been free from responsibility, and I was leaving it. Or was that the real reason for my feeling this way? Was it that I wouldn't see the doctor again? Then I remembered that I was to see him. I was going to make trips to see him every two weeks at the Baxter County Health Center. I also remembered the shock treatments and was glad I was on my way home. I still felt troubled, remembering the nurse or attendant saying just before I passed out for that last treatment, "Oh, My!" What had gone wrong to make her say that? I would probably never know.

Chapter 3

Aftermath

After Phil took me home, he went on to River City to work, and, except for Henry and Mark, I was alone. By noon, however, my folks had come down bringing the two girls home. When Dad took a notion to do something, he did it right now. No doubt he was wondering about me and couldn't wait. Phil would probably have to go after the two boys.

It didn't take me long to realize there was something wrong with me. My emotions were in a churning turmoil. I was all mixed up and acting strangely. I'd cry at something funny and laugh at something sad. I was laughing and crying at intervals over nothing. I seemed to know I was acting crazy, and I'd cry about that. My folks didn't say anything, but I was sure I noticed a puzzled expression on Mama's face. Nevertheless, they went home and left the two girls with me.

Since I had a car to drive now, I drove it every place the rest of the week. But, whereas before I'd been overly cautious, I was now reckless. I drove too fast and turned corners without judgment. Once, when I turned a corner too fast and the car door flew open and almost spilled the kids, I only laughed. They must have been frightened but were too scared to say anything. At the end of the week, when Phil came home and learned how I'd been acting, he was angry. He was sure it was caused from the shock treatments, but why hadn't Dr. Banks warned us? He took me to see Dr. Jackson, and he also thought we should have known about it. He let the car stay home anyway, so I could drive it to see Dr. Banks. By that time, my confusion had cleared up some. I told Dr. Banks that Phil and Dr. Jackson weren't too pleased that they hadn't been warned about my goofy actions. He again sat in a comfortable position and didn't say anything. I wondered what I should say, since he evidently wasn't going to talk. I imagined he was waiting for me to "start talking," but that was what I wanted him to do. I wanted him to ask me some questions.

I felt scared and embarrassed and unsure of myself. What did he expect me to do? He just sat and watched me with a patient look on his face, as if waiting for me to say something. But I couldn't think of a single thing to say. My mind seemed to be a total blank. Frantically, I tried to think of something, but the harder I tried, the blanker I got. A kind of an anger was again welling up inside me. Why didn't he talk? Then I would know what to say. That was the way we sat through most of the 45 minutes, he sitting comfortably with his feet on the desk quietly and calmly waiting for me to "start talking," and I on edge and tense waiting for him to "start talking."

"Write an autobiography," he finally said when it was time for me to leave. "I want you to write seven pages of the first seven years of your life." I was to write it and have it ready when I came back in two weeks. That scared me. I worried about it all the way home. Write a story. That had been one of the worst assignments a teacher could give me when I was in school—write a 100-word theme. But this was more than a hundred words. My story writing in high school had pulled my grades down.

So I went home to worry about writing seven pages of autobiography. I could hardly remember anything that happened during my first seven years. I must rely on what I had been told. I knew I had been born in a log house in Montana. I could remember something about riding on trains. I could remember a little about going to school and about my little brother who died with flu and pneumonia when he was two and I was six. It had been in the winter of 1919-20. I could remember something about my uncle who had gone to war. Every aeroplane, I thought, meant the "Kizy" was coming. I'd been so afraid of so many things. But seven pages—I had a sinking feeling.

Besides that worry, I worried about the amnesia that seemed to have come over me, knowing it was from the ECT. But I forgot such crazy things. I'd hear the name of a small town I knew was nearby, but I couldn't place it. Was it north? Or south? Or east? Or west? I couldn't even remember where a town only five or six miles away was located. I felt terribly silly when someone told me where it was.

About two weeks after I came home from the hospital and my folks had brought the girls home, they came down again, but I couldn't remember their being there the other time.

"It's sure been a long time since you've been here," I said to Mama. "I haven't seen you all summer."

She looked surprised and said, "Why, we were just down here two weeks ago!"

It dawned on me she was right, and I began to cry. My brain cells wore destroyed. After chewing my pencil for two weeks and pacing the floor and writing really big, I finally got my seven pages. In the meantime, Dr. Banks had written to Dr. Jackson and explained to him that my confusion was caused from the ECT and would clear up in about two weeks. So by now my emotions had sort of calmed down, but I still felt the amnesia. I had trouble placing towns and trying to remember who a person was when I heard their name.

Again, the doctor just sat and seemed to be waiting for me to talk. I couldn't think of a word to say, and my anxiety grew. I sat and sat and sat, getting tenser by the minute, until I could take it no longer and suddenly blurted out in anger, "Why don't you say something?"

He just shrugged and said, unconcernedly, "It's your time; do what you want with it." Then, after 45 minutes, he shook hands and told me to write 14 pages of my next seven years.

While sitting in the room with Dr. Banks, I'd felt anxious and scared and angry, but when I left the building and was on my way home, that strange attraction came over me. I felt as if I wanted to go back to the Health Center and see him some more. I felt guilty. I must fight it, I thought. It was that something called rapport I tried to console myself, but I wouldn't be consoled. I must fight it. At the same time thoughts of Sherlock Holmes would flash through my head at intervals.

I spent another two weeks working and worrying about the fourteen pages of autobiography I was to write along with my other work. Yet, I found the fourteen pages easier to get than the seven pages.

One day, Phil and I were in town and ran into a friend. She talked to Phil and practically ignored me. I didn't give it too much thought, thinking that she'd probably gotten engrossed in what they were talking about.

But a few days later, when we went to town and saw her again, and she did the very same thing, I knew something was wrong. She evidently wasn't angry with Phil, but what had I done to her to make her act like that? It had me stumped.

"I can't figure her out," I told Caroline. "I know she's mad at me about something, but I don't know what. She didn't act mad at Daddy, and if she's mad at one of us, she's usually mad at both of us. I couldn't have done anything to her recently, because I haven't seen her all summer."

"You have, too, Mama," Caroline said. "She came to see you the next day after you came home from the hospital."

"She did?" I asked. To save my life, I couldn't remember it. "Where was I when she was here?" I asked, after studying on it for several minutes.

"Out milking the cows," Caroline filled me in.

It was sort of coming back to me, but I still didn't have a clear picture of it. What would milking the cows have to do with her getting angry at me? Still puzzled, I asked, "What did I do or say?"

"Nothing," she said. "You just bragged."

Gradually the mystery began to clear. I was beginning to remember. I knew now what I'd done. Even though I liked the friend, she did like to brag. Her chickens, her cows, her kids, her sheep and everything she had was better than everybody else's. When she did, I had always tensed up and listened, but suddenly my inhibitions had left me. ECT had done it. I laughed. I was really making up for lost time.

My trips to see the psychiatrist became more and more important all the time. It was a must that I go, but when I sat in the room with him, I felt tense and unsure of myself. After that time when I jumped him about talking, he tried to do more of it, but he still seemed to sit back and let me take the initiative. It was hard for me to do. I wanted him to take the lead. But he'd just sit in a comfortable position with his feet on the desk and looking relaxed. Sometimes I would feel a little spurt of anger well up inside me, but I'd say nothing about it.

Every so often he would pop a critical remark at me about my grooming. It still wasn't easy for me. Milking cows and playing nursemaid to my ewes in lambing season and building fires and plowing corn weren't exactly conducive to good grooming. Besides, it bothered me to put on lipstick and fool with my hair and my fingernails. Dad had been terribly against women primping, and I felt guilty just to look in a mirror.

I still couldn't understand my feeling of attraction for the doctor when he could be so critical and make me feel all tense and guilty. I was sure he was at least ten years younger than I was and had a wife. I had always been able to have my writing assignment finished and ready for him, with the correct number of sheets, even if they might have been in big letters so I wouldn't have to get so many words on a page. But each time he increased the number, and finally the time came when I went home, and, in spite of chewing my pencil to a pulp, I couldn't even put one word down. I'd pace the floor and then put my paper away, thinking maybe I can write something later. Later nothing came. I had nothing for the doctor when I went back to see him. It didn't seem to bother him; however, he shortened my assignment for the next time. Evidently, he was in no pushing hurry.

In spite of his criticism of my grooming and a growing tendency for him to mock me about my "eating worms," as he called it, or getting sarcastic about my wanting sympathy or not fighting for my rights, he did seem to have some faith in my abilities. He thought I was smart, and I didn't think I was dumb, but intelligence and talent were two different things, I believed. I had no talent for anything—music, art, writing or talking. I was a failure as a teacher, a mother and even a hired girl.

One week while loading bulls on a boxcar to be shipped out to New York, Phil was hurt when a huge black Angus turned on him, crushing his knee. When Phil got out of the hospital, he came home to stay. He couldn't drive the car, but he could go along with me to watch Cynthia and Edward while I talked to the doctor. I could see the car in the parking lot through the picture window. At the same time, Phil could see us inside, and one day on the way home, Phil said, "What do you and Dr. Banks have to talk about so interesting? I can see you gesture and laugh and talk." I hadn't realized we had been doing that. I usually felt so tense, but perhaps I was getting more relaxed with him at times, anyway.

The next time I went back to see Dr. Banks, I told him what Phil had said, and without a word he got up and walked over to the window and pulled the Venetian blinds shut.

Nevertheless, the doctor continued to be downright insulting at times. He'd mock me like a smart-aleck boy mocking his sister. His sarcasm stung. I'd feel hurt, and a surge of anger would come over me, but I'd hold my tongue.

In time, however, I got a little braver, and my anger would come out. One day while I was telling him something while he sat leaned back in his chair with his eyes closed and his feet on the desk, I felt a sudden anger come over me. He was sleeping, I thought. I stopped what I was saying and snapped angrily, "You're asleep; you haven't heard a word I said."

"I heard every word you said," he said quietly. He then repeated my words just as I had said them.

I also began to wonder if he was really reading my autobiography, or was he just having me do it for exercise? As I got nearer and nearer the end, it got easier and easier to write. He now said, "You don't have to write it so completely, now. Just skim over it and write the main things." So, I thought, he's getting tired of reading it.

"You're not even reading this," I told him angrily.

"I do too," he said, without seeming to get angry. "I read every word of it before I leave."

I finally finished it. Toward the last of the year, Phil went back to work, actually before he was ready and immediately slipped on the cement floor and broke his wrist. He was home a while longer. When he did go back, I had to keep one of the school kids home from school to go with me. This didn't please the teachers, but I could see nothing else to do. I felt I must see the doctor. I took turns, however, and kept one kid home one time and another one the next time.

Maybe the reason these trips to see the doctor became so all-important to me was that it mostly made up my social life. Except for my stopping at a neighbor's while hunting for my fence-crawling cows or an occasional school affair like a mother-daughter banquet or a commencement exercise, I had very little social life. If I went to church, I would come home and pace the floor, because when I would try to give my opinion of something, the others would look at me as if I were an atheist, which I definitely was not. Then I would go to church determined to keep still and let the others have their say, but I would still come home upset. I would hear the others make statements that seemed so illogical. So many people were so steeped in tradition, even though that church criticized others for relying on tradition. People felt about their religion the way they felt about their dog—I don't care if my dog is a hound, you quit kicking my dog around.

"You were unfortunately born with a high IQ," Dr. Banks said to me once, as if intelligence was a liability rather than an asset. Maybe I saw his point.

One day I happened to glance toward his feet, which he had crossed and on the desk. I was surprised and quickly looked away. He was wearing unmatched socks. If it had been one of my boys, I might have been surprised to see them wearing matched socks. But this was different. Dr. Banks was so persnickety, I thought. He was always criticizing me for my poor grooming. Surely, he must know that wearing socks of different colors wasn't exactly good grooming. I felt confused and didn't look at his feet again. My thinking seemed muddled for a while, and I hardly knew what was going on around me. In time, however, I sort of came out of the spell and seemed to forget about the socks. Yet, I must have been thinking of them subconsciously, because I never once looked toward his feet again that day.

On the way home, however, thoughts of the socks started creeping into my thinking. For a couple of miles, I rode in silence, trying to get the mystery cleared up. There must be an answer. I remembered the psychiatrist who had yelled at me just to get my reaction. I knew, now, that he had put it all on. Was that the answer? Had Dr. Banks worn those socks to see what I would do? Would I have nerve enough to call him on it? That's it, I thought. The more I thought about it, the more I was convinced I had stumbled onto the doctor's little trick. So, he thought he'd fooled me, did he? The more sure I was that I had the right answer, the funnier it got. I began to laugh. I thought some more and laughed harder. It was hard for me to drive the car for thinking about the socks and laughing. Well, I thought, he's not going to get by with this. I'll sure tell him about it next time.

But when the next time came, I lost my nerve. I saw no sign that he might have something up his sleeve. There was nothing about his actions that might indicate he was expecting me to assert myself. I began to wonder if I had been seeing things, but when I was on the way home again, I began to study it again. I again became convinced I'd been right all the time. He had done it deliberately. I'll tell him about it next time. The same thing happened the next time. While in the room with him, I'd lose my nerve, but on the way home my confidence would return, and I'd promise myself I'd tell him the next time. Then, I began to wonder if I'd seen right, and if he really had been wearing unmatched socks. Had my eyes deceived me? Why had I refused to look at his feet after that initial look that day? I now felt angry at myself. I'd been sure then. I was getting more and more fearful to tell him about it. Suppose it was true, but it had been an accident. Would he be embarrassed if I called him on it? I didn't really want to do that, although he didn't mind embarrassing me by accusing me of eating worms and such. Gradually, the sock incident seem to dwindle and become unimportant. I gave up trying to tell him about it.

He still seemed to have a lot of faith in me. I'd say "I can't," and he'd say "You can." We'd yell at each other for several minutes, just saying I can't, you can, I can't, you can. Finally, I'd give up and let him have the last word. But he had me confounded. He could be so kind at times and so ornery and sarcastic at other times.

Chapter 4

Coping

Whatever the psychiatrist was doing for me, he wasn't solving my home problems. In fact, that didn't seem to be his purpose. I guessed he was trying to work on my problems with myself so I could solve my other problems without his help. But then, my problem with Toby was a rough one.

Toby never had liked school since the first day, when he had come running home as fast as his legs could carry him. He had been let out for the first recess and had already decided that school wasn't for him. I saw him coming and was there to meet him and took him by the hand and led him back to school. Now he was a freshman and still didn't like school. He'd always been my most active kid from the time he had taken his first step at nine months—even before. After he started high school, he began to play hooky now and then with another boy. I begged and scolded and talked and tried to reason with him. I think I did hold him down some, but he still wouldn't study.

The trouble was that I seemed to be getting no cooperation from the school—especially from the hot-headed principal. He made no attempt to try to understand Toby, I thought. His attitude was that Toby was no good and he didn't want to fool with him. *[Note: I don't understand this. Apparently, I was oblivious to all these sessions with the principal and superintendent, or I have forgotten it, but I remember something the math teacher told me. He said that Toby was the smartest student he had in the freshman algebra class and that Toby helped the other students who were having trouble with algebra. I couldn't understand, however, why Toby kept bringing home F's in algebra on his grade card. I have heard of kids adding a bottom leg on an F to make it look like an E. (We had the ESMIF grading system.) Do you suppose he was erasing the bottom leg of an E? That sounds crazy, but he was that much of a maverick. Through all these years I have never thought to ask him about that. Mom is not exaggerating about the fact that he marched to a different drummer. Today, he probably would be diagnosed as ADHD and put on Ritalin. Who knows what a difference that would have made. Caroline.]*

The superintendent was a much more reasonable man, but he seemed ready to stand behind his teachers, no matter what. It was impossible for a teacher to do any wrong. If there was any trouble, it was entirely the parent's fault. I had taught and knew of some of the teacher's problem. Teachers shouldn't be blamed for everything, either. Neither should parents. They are both human, and both could be wrong. Teachers have their faults as well as the parents.

I wanted my kids to finish high school. I'd had my problems with the others at times, but it looked as if Mark would finally finish. He only had a few months to go. But now it seemed Toby might not, if I didn't get any help from the school. I was ready to do anything to keep him going. Like the old saying "you can lead a horse to water, but you can't make him drink," you can send a kid to school, but you can't make him like it. How, I wondered, could they expect the kid to like school when the teacher showed his dislike for the boy so strongly? If only the school had a psychologist—or someone—to help straighten out the rift between the teacher and the boy. I went to Mrs. Gray, but, again, we weren't eligible since we weren't on welfare.

Help! I wanted help. Where could I send out an SOS? No place. I had to do it alone. Not even Phil was home enough to help me much. I knew Toby's trouble hadn't started in high school. For years my kids had been discriminated against— even in the small country school. I knew much of it had been my fault. I couldn't fight for their rights. Other parents, I was sure, would have gone to the school and worked it over from top to bottom if their children had been treated the way mine had. This, I supposed, was what Dr. Banks called my "eating worms". I wasn't a fighter.

There was one teacher I liked a lot and she did much for my kids, especially for Mark, who had given me some trouble in his early years, partly no doubt, from his almost having a nervous breakdown when I had mine. She made one bad mistake, however, and I let her get by with it. Every morning, she had a health inspection, and the children conducted it, with very little—if any—supervision from her. The kids took turns being inspector, but if they got a black mark, they couldn't have their turn. Time after time, my kids were passed over and never got their turn. Every day they got a black mark. They'd scrub for 30 minutes before they went to school, and I'd inspect them, but still they'd get a mark. Sometimes they'd come home crying. They'd scrub harder the next day. They got their black marks while the others never got any. One day one boy did get one, and he cried. The teacher said, "He might have gotten it after he got to school." He wasn't given the mark. The other kids seemed to think that if they found no dirt on my kids they hadn't done their duty. *[Note: I know this all sounds like a paranoid exaggeration, but everything she says here is absolutely true. I don't know that we were that much poorer than the other families in the school, but we were a large family with a very poorly-kept house, so we were at the bottom of the social pecking order. What really rankled them was that our mental abilities did not fall into line with that order. They couldn't stand it that we were smarter than any of them, so they had to put us in our place in other ways. As for the teacher, suffice it to say that my parents never did serve on the school board. She knew which side her bread was buttered on, so to speak. Caroline.]*

I didn't blame the kids for all of it. The teacher was definitely to blame. I was sure the kids' parents also had something to do with it. They'd heard their parents talk at home. They had ignored my working in the field and had gossiped about my house. My spells of depression had been another thing that made the kids believe it was impossible for there to be anything good about my kids. But why punish the kids for my trouble? Besides, mine would come home and tell how they would yank on their ears and treat them roughly, when they'd just walk by the others and not even touch them. I was sure that my kids had no more dirt than the others. Finally, Toby had come home and angrily said, "I'm never going to wash my face as long as I live."

What had the teacher accomplished by her inspection? Only give the kids a feeling of discouragement and antagonism toward school and rules and laws, I thought. Week after week and month after month and year after year of this was bound to have an adverse effect on the kid's attitude.

I was sure things like that were having some influence on Toby's not liking school now. It might not be the whole story, but it was part of it. Now Toby's high school teachers were saying it was all the parents' fault. We turned the kids over to the school when they were six and from then on, the school had them six or seven hours out of the day. Why shouldn't the school take some of the responsibility? Discriminating against the kids in school certainly didn't help them any. I wasn't blaming it all on the teachers, but at least they could help me. Finally we gave up on Toby, and, in collaboration with the superintendent, we let Toby quit and go back to work on the dairy farm where he'd worked the summer before. Work was better than nothing.

Another time, Dr. Banks had asked me point-blank how I felt about him, but I tried to act dumb and pretend I hadn't understood what he meant. Had he seen some of my feelings and wanted to get them out in the open? Yet, I couldn't seem to talk about it—not yet anyway. I'd handle those feelings myself. Besides, it wasn't important, and what could he do if I told him? It was normal for women to fall in love with their psychiatrist, wasn't it? It wasn't love, anyway, I reasoned.

In spite of these strong feelings for Dr. Banks, I also had the opposite feelings. I couldn't quite get over his having given me ECT. Although almost a year had passed since I'd had the treatments, I still had spells of amnesia. I still would feel stumped if I heard the name of a town not far away, trying to locate it. There was no doubt in my mind; the treatments did permanent damage to the brain cells. I would feel terribly angry with him at times.

I never had told him about my feeling, or perhaps it was a sensation, that he was Sherlock Holmes. But one day he said, "I'm Dr. Banks. I'm your doctor and nobody else." He must have sensed that I was linking him with someone else besides himself.

Sometimes I'd remember hearing the nurse say, just before I had taken my last treatment, "Oh! My!" I wondered what had caused her to say it. Had something gone wrong? Had they turned on more electricity than they had meant to? Was that the reason the hospital had made me stay a little longer? Was that the reason my amnesia had seemed so severe? It was a mystery, I knew, that would probably never be answered. Another mystery was why did some things like that remain such a vivid picture in my mind, and other things I couldn't remember? Why should I forget where towns were located and remember that? Why should I forget the faces of people when I heard their names?

In spite of my resentments and the doctor's sarcasm, my dependence on him seemed to grow. Was it that he was making me feel like something besides some of the livestock or a piece of furniture? Was he creating some spunk in me? Was I feeling more like something besides a chair that had no feelings of its own and was just something to be used for someone's comfort?

Caroline was spending the summer between her junior and senior years in River City with Phil trying to get summer work there. One Sunday, Phil and Caroline came home. Toby wanted some of his clothes brought up to him. It was a 150 mile trip, and most of it would have to be done at night. There would be no time to stay. "Caroline can go along and drive part of the way if I get sleepy," Phil said. She was 17 and had her driver's license now. A sudden desire to go came over me. I had a driver's license too.

"I'll go," I said.

"You can't," he said.

"Why can't I go?" I asked. "I can drive, too."

"You have to stay home to milk the cows and take care of the livestock."

"The kids can do that. They're old enough."

"They can't do all of it." Caroline hadn't done much milking, but Chuck had. It would only be that one night, and maybe we'd be home in time to do it in the morning.

"What about Cynthia and Edward?"

"Caroline is 17; she's old enough to care for them one night." The idea of going was getting more desirable all the time. Why was he so determined for me not to go. He saw me as a piece of furniture. I was just like the livestock.

"Why are you so set on going? It wouldn't be any fun for you. We won't have any time to stay and visit any."

"I don't care. I just want to go along for the ride."

"That's silly. It'll be dark and you can't see anything."

"I just want to go."

"You're just like a little kid," he said.

That did it. It was too much for me to take. I was hurt clear through. I stayed home all week long and kept the home fires burning, and he could accuse me of being just like a little kid. So many times in the past he had taken long trips, and I couldn't go along. His dad had owned some land in Louisiana for speculation, and Phil had made several trips down there while I stayed home. Maybe I couldn't see anything, and maybe I couldn't visit, but just to get away for a few hours was something. Caroline was away all week long and could go to a show or whatever, but I was tied down.

When I was a kid, I remember Dad taking the same attitude with Mama. She stayed home and never went anyplace while Dad went to town and got the groceries and talked to men, but he never seemed to realize Mama needed to get away. I remember once when I was about ten, she had taken all the kids and walked two miles to a neighbor, and when he came home and found her gone, he was furious. I was mad. Now Phil was doing the same thing to me, although his mother had been different and had gone wherever she wanted to go. I let him do it.

Usually in a case like this I would have given up and let Phil have his way. Caroline would have gone, and I would have stayed home. I might develop a depression and my head would again fill with cotton, and I couldn't think straight. Dr. Banks would accuse me of eating worms if he heard about it. But for some reason, this time I made up my mind I was going even if Phil did think I was like a little kid for wanting to go. I stuck it out, and when Phil was ready, I got in the car with him. I doubted that Caroline cared much whether she went or not. It was all Phil's idea, anyway.

It couldn't have been called a pleasure trip. We drove most of the way in silence. I cried, and Phil pouted. He had called me a little kid. I was hurt and mad. Why? Why? Why? I couldn't understand it. I was nothing but a piece of furniture. Phil saw me as something useful. I was something to leave at home and be there always. I wasn't a human. I wasn't a woman. I thought of Dr. Banks. He was trying to tell me I was something else. He was making me feel like something else. That's why I felt about him the way I did. He was trying to make me think of myself as a human. As a woman. That's why this crazy feeling for the doctor kept coming over me.

Why couldn't Phil see what he was doing to me? I didn't want to feel that way about the doctor. He was just a doctor. I knew that. I knew who he was. It wasn't love I felt for him. It was just that dependence I felt for him. Even if I could have, I didn't want to trade Phil for him. Phil was the father of all my babies. No one could take that place. I had a genuine liking for the doctor, but it wasn't love. I couldn't help it. I had no control over my feelings, but I might not feel this way if Phil treated me differently. Why couldn't he see? He was good-natured in lots of ways, but he had that same old-fashioned idea about women that Dad had. But it was different with Dad. Dad had come out of it when his children were grown. Years ago lots of men felt that way about their women. Men owned women. Women were property. But not now. I cried, and Phil still pouted. He was like his mother. He wouldn't argue. He'd sit and pout and not say anything. He was so sure he was right. I was wrong. If we could only talk our differences out, but he seemed to think there was no need to discuss it. He made no attempt at starting. Always when we had a spat—or whatever it was—I'd have to start. And it wasn't easy.

It was no use. If we talked, I'd have to be the one to start it. Otherwise, we'd be just where we started. In time, we'd both get over this, but I'd still be the old piece of furniture. I had to make him understand. I had to make him know what he was doing to me. How long could I keep this up? Would it end in a divorce? I didn't want a divorce. I didn't believe in them. They never solved anything. I must make him understand.

Finally, I made a start. But he showed no signs of trying to help me out. Yet, I had to. I tried some more, and still he said very little. Why should we talk about it? seemed to be his thoughts. You're wrong and that's final. He wouldn't even try. I remembered what Caroline had said one time about my acting as if I were in love with the doctor. "You know, when Caroline said I acted like being in love with Dr. Banks. In a way she was right."

Even that didn't wake him up. He was so self-righteous. I went on, "But it doesn't mean anything. It's something called rapport, I think. I don't really love him. It's just that he makes me feel like something besides an old rocking chair. Or a stove or a table. Or even like one of the cows. You don't. I'm only something to keep things going at home."

Gradually Phil began to come out of his shell and answered me. I didn't know for sure whether he was following me or not, but he appeared to be. I tried to make him understand I wasn't trying to ditch him for the doctor. I was just a patient to him. It was just a feeling. If he'd only treat me a little differently.

By the time we reached our destination, I was feeling some better, and I guessed Phil was. The woman made us come in and eat something and drink some coffee. I didn't get a chance to see any of my family, but we did visit a while with her. I think when we got home I was feeling a lot better. Maybe the trip helped after all.

In July, Phil's dad passed away after a brief illness. A neighbor man's mother also died. He seemed unable to get over it and would come over to our place when Phil was home, or even when he wasn't, and talk and talk about it. I thought about that—the difference in the way the two men were taking it. Phil had been terribly close to his dad. Why did the other man take it so much harder? So many times I sat and huddled while friends and relatives would preach to me about how somebody else had the same things happen to them, and they never took it like I did. Was there a difference? There were times when I'd see someone else having the "blues," and I'd tell my lecturers about it, wondering why they could feel blue and there was nothing wrong with it, but when I felt blue, I was such a sinner. They'd say, "That's different; they have a reason, but you don't." That statement baffled me; I saw no difference.

Now, I saw the difference in the way Phil and the neighbor were taking the death of a parent. I thought, there is a difference. Maybe I couldn't see it, but there had to be a difference. There was a reason. I remembered Mama getting slightly aggravated with me once when I told her there was a reason for everything. She told me in an irritable voice that I was just like Kenneth, who was my brother 12 years younger than I. He was always saying there was a reason for everything, too. That's right, I thought, there is a reason for everything. There was a reason for the neighbor man taking the death of his mother so hard. It might be obscure to the rest of us, but there was a reason. I thought about my thinking of Dr. Banks as the famous detective, Sherlock Holmes, and what was behind my thinking that way. There must be a reason for that, also. Did Dr. Banks look like I had Sherlock Holmes pictured? Or was it something in me?

Was it my seeming to identify him with Holmes that caused him to say, "Most of the time, you react negatively to me. Once in a while, you react positively to me." I'd been thinking I was reacting too positively toward him. One time, I went to see him anyway in spite of a bad case of poison ivy with watery blisters all over my arms. Usually I'd get a series of three shots from Dr. Jackson in the spring, but I must have neglected it that year. The shots helped, although all summer I'd seem to have a slight itching all over my body. Still, that was better than the poison ivy blisters. Dr. Banks didn't say anything about it that day, but the next time I went to see him and it was all cleared up, he accused me of getting the poison ivy on purpose to make him feel sorry for me. I was hurt, and I was furious, but I couldn't convince him I had done nothing of the sort. The idea that I'd get into the stuff on purpose was crazy. My getting his sympathy couldn't possibly compensate for the misery it caused me. "You could have kept from getting into it," he insisted. But that wasn't as easy as he might imagine, with a big ditch the full length of the farm.

I didn't take him too seriously when he told me I should go to college. "I'm too old," I said.

"My mother went to college when she was older than you," he said.

"I don't have the money to go to college."

"I know a person, who will loan the money to anyone if he is satisfied it will help the person."

"What about my kids? Who will take care of them? It takes money to hire a baby sitter."

"I believe the money for that would be available, also."

I never gave that suggestion of his too much thought. When I graduated from high school, it never entered my mind that

I might go to college, even when the neurotic woman whose back I rubbed told me I had a scholarship coming to me, but I would have to go and ask them for it. I hadn't been so sure I did and didn't have the courage to go. Anyway, it wasn't for me the woman was wanting it. She had said, "You get it and let me use it; I'll pay you a little bit for it." I wasn't so sure it could be transferred to someone else, and if it could be, it wouldn't be right. It still never dawned on me that I might use it myself. Only rich people's kids went to college.

The thought of my going to college was just as preposterous now as it was then. If I was a failure as a teacher then, what would make me a success now, I thought, when he suggested I try to teach after my asking what I should study to try to be. Since the idea seemed so silly, I just forgot it.

One day he was discussing my having so many children. He said, "Now if you were a moron, it would he all right for you to have a house full of kids."

"You mean a house full of little morons, don't you?" I asked, and he didn't answer me.

My kids were far from morons. Caroline got the highest grades in her class, and in the IQ tests the school gave, the scores my kids got were high. My boys wouldn't study, but their scores on the standardized tests and such were way up there.

In the fall, when school started, Caroline came home to finish her last year. Chuck was ready for high school. Toby also came home after his boss had convinced him he should finish high school. He really wanted to go to school, I thought.

Phil stayed home that first morning, so he could go to school with Toby and talk to the principal or the superintendent. I was genuinely worried when Phil returned, leaving Toby at school, and told me what had taken place. They had talked to the principal. He wasn't very enthusiastic about having Toby come back. After agreeing, reluctantly, to allow Toby to return to school, he said, "You can come back, but we don't expect much from you."

Phil said to me, "I don't know whether Toby caught it or not. He didn't say anything about it, and I kept still. I hope Toby didn't hear him say that, or if he did, he didn't get the implication. If he did, I'm afraid things won't work out."

I was afraid of that too. But what could we do? Only sit and hold our breath, hoping for the best, even if it was an unrealistic thought. I was sick. How could a teacher make that kind of remark and call himself a teacher?

Things went along fairly well for awhile. I was beginning to think that Toby had missed what the principal had said. It wasn't long, however, before Toby again took a notion of playing hooky. I found it out and tried to get him to go. But he and another boy had made plans to go fishing, and he wouldn't let the other boy down. I coaxed and begged and pleaded with him, but he had made up his mind. Then it came out. "Mr. Randolph hates me. He doesn't want me to come to school. He said he didn't expect anything from me the first day of school."

There it was. He hadn't missed it after all. I had no answer for him. He was only fifteen and by law was supposed to be in school, but I couldn't handle him the way I had about ten years before when I'd led him by the hand. He was tall—about six feet. So he set out against my will. What could I do? Was there no one to help me? I called the school and talked to Mr. Randolph. He made it plain from the first he didn't care whether Toby came to school or not. His job was to teach and that was all. It was all the parents' fault, he insisted, when a kid did things like that. He talked to me as if I were a criminal—as though I'd deliberately gone out of my way to keep my boy from going, but I'd gone out of my way to keep him going. I knew there were parents who made little attempt to keep their kids in school, but I wasn't one of them. I finally gave up on the principal and talked to the superintendent. He talked better than the principal had, but he still was going to do nothing against his teachers. He would back his teachers to the hilt. He, like the principal, seemed to place all the blame on the parents. Perhaps I hadn't always done a perfect job raising my kids, but I'd done the best I could with all the interference I'd had. Would these teachers have taken the same attitude if Phil had been a banker or a druggist or some important man in the neighborhood? Most parents, I thought, did the best they could. Some might be hampered by education or intelligence or illness or poverty, but was that a reason for not giving the kid a chance?

"Is he unruly in the classroom?" I finally asked the superintendent. I might have understood why they didn't want him in school. "Does he cause trouble or dissension?"

"No," he said, "it's nothing like that."

Then why? Why wouldn't the school help me? I was lost. Toby had come back with the best of intentions, I was sure. He really wanted to finish high school. Yet, what could a person expect when the school told him they didn't want him, that they expected nothing from him. Suddenly, I blew up. I was furious. I said heatedly, "Mr. Randolph expected the worst from Toby, and that's exactly what he got—the worst."

After that, he calmed down some and talked a little more reasonably. Still, I must find some way to get my boy to go to school. Where could I go? I couldn't go to Mrs. Gray, because we weren't on welfare. Where then? Didn't they have a truant officer, I began to wonder. I asked around and found out that since the country schools had been discontinued, so had the need for a county superintendent been disposed of. But, I learned, he still had a job. He was now the truant officer. So I took Toby to him. He was firm but seemed to be understanding. Toby made several trips to see him and talk to him. What he did, I never knew, but Toby did stop playing hooky.

Chapter 5

Nowhere to Turn to

In September when we made the trip to Iowa, I was a little worried about Mama. She was still up and going, but she was having trouble sleeping unless she sat in a chair. Her hands didn't look right, I thought. They looked so blue. I told her she'd better go to the doctor, and she agreed she would.

Then in October she died after being in the hospital for just a short while. She had diabetes, but it was her heart that caused her death. At the funeral, I felt so funny, and I was unable to understand why. I had such a detached feeling. In the coffin, she looked so natural, too, but it was as if she were a stranger. It's not normal, I thought. It's unnatural not to feel a certain amount of grief. What's wrong with me? I felt guilty. I couldn't even feel she was dead. Maybe it'll come later, I reasoned. But it didn't, not even during the services. It wasn't necessary to get hysterical, but this was terrible to feel this way. Something was wrong with me.

Gradually a thought began to form in my mind; I knew what was wrong with me. The shock treatments had destroyed some important brain cells. ECT had done this to me. It had made me into a robot. I was sub-human. Some wires had been cut, and I couldn't feel normal grief. This was worse than the amnesia, I thought. A feeling of anger came over me toward Dr. Banks. He had turned me into a robot.

I never told this to him, but I did complain about the amnesia now and then, at which he only said, "If you can't remember something, it's because you don't want to remember it."

Then I said something about the housework bothering me. He passed it off with, "The reason you can't do your housework is because you just don't like to do it. It's not enough of a challenge to your intellect." I was sure he was wrong about that. There was something else involved that caused the tension to build up when I did it other than just not making me think. I told him about not being able to throw things away and that things got piled up. He told me the story about the man who went to see the psychiatrist because he liked pancakes too well.

"That's nothing," the psychiatrist said. "I like pancakes, too."

"That's fine," the man replied. "Come over some time, and we'll have some. I have trunks and trunks full of them." Dr. Banks said I reminded him of that story.

One day a depression seemed to be building, and I couldn't stop thinking. Phil had the habit of telling me to stop thinking, but it never did any good. The neighbors were talking about me because of my house. I was a piece of furniture. I was no good. I can't. The thoughts rolled over and over in my head.

Dr. Banks called me a masochist. He said I wanted to he punished. But I didn't. He said that I let people get the best of me because I liked it, and that I enjoyed having people talk me down. It wasn't true. For some reason I couldn't seem to fight for my rights. Then if I did and won, I'd feel guilty. It was no use; I couldn't win. I was a born loser. I got lower and lower. Get away from it all. Go away where no one could find me. Where? New York. How could I make a living? Get a job. What about the kids? Take the two small ones with me. Leave the older ones with Phil. New York was too big. St. Louis. Kansas City. But I knew nothing about city life. I would be scared.

Then there was the matter of living. If I got lost, I would have nothing to eat. Besides, how could I work if I had the kids to care for? Anyway, what made me think I could get work when I was such a failure? My head was getting stuffier and stuffier. I couldn't think straight. My head was stuffed with cotton. Could I leave the two babies, too? No! Phil would have to quit his job to take care of them. Then there was the farm. It would be gone. If Phil had to take care of the kids, he couldn't work and couldn't keep the farm. Everything would be gone—my horses, my cows, my sheep. No other sheep could take the place of my pets. Little Iodine with the black face—the black sheep of the family and the mischief-maker. Jean and Babe, my old faithful work team, would be gone. I might get homesick and come home, but they would all be gone. It would be too late. But I had to do something; I couldn't take this much longer. What couldn't I take? I didn't know. Go! Go! Go! Leave it all. The word whirled and whirled in my head. The kids could make it. I'm no good to them anyway. Maybe I could make it by myself. Where? Again the thoughts of New York and St. Louis and all the big cities in the nation.

How could I give all this up? I loved the farm. I had lived on a farm all my life. I could never make it in a large city, alone. We would lose everything we had worked for. I would be sure to come back sooner or later. No, that wasn't the answer. Where? If I left and went far away and got lost, I couldn't go and see Dr. Banks. Go to the city, where he had his office. I would still have to give up the farm. Go to River City with Phil. That's what Dr. Banks wanted me to do. I would still have to give up the livestock.

But I couldn't take this. I couldn't stand up under the pressure. Too much work. Build fence. I had to depend on an electric fence a lot. The fences were poor. Hunt where the electricity was shorted out. Throw down hay to the animals. Get up ten or twenty times a night to call Buster to make sure he was there. If there were any sheep killed in the neighborhood, it was always my dog that did it, even though no one had seen the dog. Not once did my dog fail to come when I called him. How could he be out killing sheep when he was curled up in my haystack?

Fuss with the kids for an hour to make sure they didn't miss the school bus. This was different from getting them off to the small country school three-quarters of a mile away. Then drink cup after cup of coffee. My head felt bigger and bigger. I couldn't work. I couldn't do anything. I couldn't think straight. My head felt as if it were stuffed with cotton. Think. Make a decision. I can't take it and I can't leave it. Phil had no idea what it was like to be in my shoes. I felt angry at him, but what good would it do to fight with him?

Dr. Banks. He might have an answer, if there is such a thing. Or would he? What could he do? He might give me some courage. Go and see him. But my appointment wouldn't be until another week. He had skipped the last week because he had gone to the hospital to have an operation on his shoulder. He should be out of the hospital now. I couldn't wait another whole week. I had to see him now. I didn't know what I expected him to do, but it made no difference. I was sure he would make me feel better. I must see him this week, I thought.

So, when Phil came home, I told him to call the psychiatrist. It would do no good, he told me. He didn't want to do it. I insisted. He still held back. I wouldn't give up. I wouldn't call him myself. I never liked to talk over the phone. I'd have to go to his office, Phil said. I knew that, but it still made no difference. I had to see him this week. Right away.

Finally, Phil gave up and called him.. He told Phil he could see me, but if I came to his office, he'd have to charge me for it. He did go to a city several miles away, however, every other week on this same deal, and I could come there this week if I wished. It wouldn't cost me anything, either, he said.

Phil agreed and stayed home the next day to take me, since the health center in that city was right in he center of the city, and it was a much larger one than where I had been going. I wouldn't try to drive in a strange large city. Even Phil had some trouble locating the place when we got there.

The health center here was in a large building, and I had to go to an upper floor to get to it. It seemed so different from the other one. I waited in a room that seemed so small in comparison with the other one. In time I was shown to a small room with a desk in it, and Dr. Banks sat behind it. A lone book lay on the desk—nothing else. Dr. Banks looked at me with an unsympathetic gaze and said, sounding angry, "What's your trouble, now?"

I tried to answer him and felt lost for words. Was he angry because I had come? I said something.

"Well, What do you expect me to do about it?" he snapped, sarcastically.

The thought struck me, really what could he do? What had I expected him to do? I tried to explain, but it all seemed to be coming out badly. Not once did he show any understanding or smile. My emotions had been all mixed up. I had been feeling terrible. Where did a person go when they were sick? If he hadn't wanted me to come, why hadn't he told Phil? He continued to talk sarcastically, making me feel like a criminal. I felt like getting up and leaving.

Suddenly I was mad. He had his arm in a sling from the operation he'd had. I knew he had planned on having it, but this was the first time I'd seen him since he'd had it done. I got madder and started to look around for something to throw at him. I saw my purse beside me. Throw it, I thought. Then I saw the book and had an urge to pick it up and sling it right at his arm. I fought down both urges. I was boiling inside.

I was still seething when it was time for me to leave. We stood up, and, to my surprise, he put out his good hand to shake hands. With a broad smile—the first one that day—and a twinkle in his eyes, he said, "I'll see you next week." I went back out to the car, where Phil and the babies were waiting for me, not quite sure of what had happened. I wasn't sure whether my trip had been a total waste or not. I tried to figure out the doctor. I wasn't even sure that I was angry at him anymore. I went home to the same old grind, but, for some reason, I seemed to have come out of my depression.

The next week at the Baxter County Health Center, he seemed the same as usual, as if nothing unusual had happened the week before. He didn't even seem angry that I'd made that extra trip to see him. He still encouraged me to go to college, but I thought he was a little unreasonable. I couldn't do a thing like that. I really had no intention of following his suggestion when I mentioned at home that the doctor wanted me to go to college. I think I understood Caroline' horror at the idea. Why, she'd be the laughing stock of the school. It was a natural teen-age reaction. *[Note: I don't remember this at all. I can't imagine that I would ever have reacted with horror at the idea of Mom going to college, and I don't know why I would have thought that I would be the laughing stock of the school. After all, I hadn't thought that I was the laughing stock because my mother had received shock treatments. I was aware of the fact that she was by far the smartest parent in the community, and I surely would have expected her to be successful in college. Caroline.]*

But when I told a friend the same thing and she said, "Oh, you couldn't go to college. You're too weak and nervous. You couldn't stand the strain. It's different from high school." I felt hurt. It was the same thing I'd heard all my life. That's the way I felt—weak and nervous.

Winter was coming on. The days were cold. I seldom got down with a cold. If one started, I usually threw it off, and it wouldn't amount to much. This time, however, it must have been the old-fashioned flu. I was sick, and it was the day for me to go and see the psychiatrist. I thought about calling the Health Center and canceling my appointment. Yet, I was determined not to let it get me down.

Maybe, I thought, the fresh air will make me feel better. Keep going, I reasoned. I went, but was almost on the verge of turning around and coming back. I kept going. The doctor seemed less harsh than usual, but when it was time to go, he said, "You go home and get in bed. Don't you ever come down here again when you're that sick."

The next time I went to see him, he accused me of coming just to make him feel sorry for me. I didn't. I was sure that wasn't the reason. Maybe it was my way of trying to prove I wasn't weak and nervous. Another time, I forgot and skipped over the appointment. I went the next week, and he wasn't there. I'd made the trip for nothing. When I went the next week, he didn't appear to be angry, but he told me I'd done it on purpose. It seemed I could do nothing accidentally.

The winter months passed. Mark had finished his basic training and had came home on leave. He had been sent to a school in Texas and finally ended up on the flight deck of the aircraft carrier, the Shangri-La. He came home again. With his bell bottom trousers and all, he was a hero to the other kids.

Toby was still in school, but I didn't know for how long. He didn't play hooky, but one day he'd say he was going to finish high school and the next, he'd say he was going to quit on his 16th birthday in April. I was hoping.

I had been feeling some better and began to feel guilty about going to the doctor. I knew I was using him as a crutch. Finally, I suggested I quit, but he doubted I was ready. I said I was using him for a crutch. "Maybe, you are, but it's like a broken leg. If you throw away the crutch too soon, you're worse off than you were in the first place."

I let it go at that. I wasn't exactly wanting to quit anyway. It was his decision, so I didn't need to feel guilty. By this time, however, I knew I had a lot of dependence on him. I gradually felt more and more relaxed while I was in the room with the doctor. One day I found myself in a heated argument with him and didn't know how it had come about. I could argue that there was no literal hell that people were thrown into to burn forever, the way most of the religions taught, but he had said Jesus was just a man, that he wasn't Christ. This was different. I believed wholehearted in Jesus as Christ. I had my reasons, and it wasn't because my mother believed and my grandmother believed and my great grandmother had believed it. I had other reasons— ones I had figured out on my own. We argued up one side and down the other, and he sat stony-faced, as if he believed what he was saying. But when it was time to go, he stood up and held out his hand to shake hands and said, with a broad smile on his face, "Now, you're living."

I had almost forgotten about the unmatched socks. Then one day I suddenly blurted out, "You played a trick on me once."

"I did? What was it?" he asked, sounding innocent.

"You know what it is," I told him, suddenly wishing I had kept still. From then on, we batted it back and forth. I wouldn't tell him, and he wouldn't admit it. He finally gave up, but I had aroused his curiosity.

February came and something went wrong with one of my wagon wheels. I didn't know how to fix it, and if I did, I probably couldn't have anyway. Phil can fix it when he comes home Sunday, I thought. Saturday night came, but Phil didn't. Sometimes, he didn't come until Sunday morning. I waited. He wasn't home at noon. I waited all afternoon. Maybe he had car trouble, I reasoned. I wanted that wheel fixed. I was getting nervous, but if he had car trouble, he couldn't help that.

Finally, he came home, but too late to fix the wheel. Then I learned what had held him up. One of the women in the apartment house where he lived was moving and wanted him to help her. So, like the Good Samaritan, he helped her. I was sick.

I didn't care if he helped her, but why did she move on the only day he was to come home. She had him right there five days a week. Why didn't she move in the morning before he went to work. She sure had her nerve. But he wasn't entirely innocent. He knew I was home and needed a little help now and then. I was mad and disgusted. I began to argue with Phil. What right did those women have to keep him from even helping his wife. I stayed on the farm all week, and they had him then to help them all he wanted to.

In time Phil said, "I think Dr. Banks is a good doctor, but I don't like him. The way you're acting is all his fault. He's trying to make you over. I like you the way you are. It's just like the difference between a show horse and a work horse. The show horse is nice to look at, but its no good for anything. I'd rather have a work horse anytime."

So, that was it. A sudden anger and hurt came over me. I was nothing but an old plug work horse. He'd wait on those city women and let me do the work. He'd roll out the red carpet for them and let me plug through the mud. He paid no attention to me. Let her work it off, seemed to be his motto. She'll get over it. When he went back to work, I couldn't get over it; he'd called me an old plug work horse. I wasn't like those poor little helpless city women. I was an old plug. All week long, I churned it around in my brain. I got lower and lower. My brain felt mushy. I felt as if cotton was in my head. Why? Why? Why?

What was the use of even trying, if that was all I was? Get away from things, again, started ringing in my head. Where? To St. Louis. To New York. I couldn't even go to see Dr. Banks this time. It would do no good. He wouldn't understand. He would say I wanted sympathy. I was sunk. There was no place.

The cotton in my head was swelling to immense proportions— pushing out, out, out. It was a tangled mess, like a sheep's wool filled with cockle burrs or sand burrs or the tangled uncurried horse's mane. It was stronger than cotton or wool or even mane. More like springs—heavy bed springs, breaking and pushing and pushing. There was no way to turn. Spoiled city women— brats. Old plug work horse.

No good. I was a failure—couldn't even teach school. Can't take care of my kids. Dr. Banks and "eating worms". Too much work. Can't leave it. No use to go the psychiatrist. He would just make fun of me. The springs pushed harder. My head was about to explode. Can't leave the farm. I didn't even have energy to commit suicide. If I did, what would become of my kids? I might be worthless, but a half a mama was better than no mama at all. I gave up. It was no use. I would just shrivel up and die.

Saturday came. Caroline was washing dishes. I had stopped fighting. Conflict. Two, three, four roads, and I couldn't figure which one to take. My head began to lose some of its pressure. My thinking started to clear up. The conflict was gone. I wasn't trying to make a decision. I remembered something.

Dad had gone to spend the winter in California, where my three brothers lived and where Amelia had also gone to live. He was coming home and was on the way. He would have to come home to an empty house. I wasn't sure just what day he would be there, but I could go to my cousin's and pick up the key and go in. This would be so much better than going to a strange city, which was ridiculous in the first place. This wouldn't be so final. I could go up there and get my thinking straightened out. I got up and started packing the babies' and my clothes.

The kids seemed to be working better than usual. They must have realized that this time I meant business. When Phil came home Sunday, I was ready for him. He didn't argue. He must have sensed I meant business also.

Leaving the other kids at home didn't worry me. Caroline was 18; Toby was almost 16; Chuck was past 14, and Henry was almost 12. They had to go to school, and the weather was nice and warm—a real spring day.

When we reached my cousin's place, I learned that Dad had already arrived. He had just come. Dad seemed glad to see me. I was killing two birds with one stone; satisfy my own feelings and save Dad from being so lonesome.

Phil left for home, and I got busy getting us something to eat and washing dishes in a sink, without having to pump and carry the water from the well. I didn't have to empty the dirty dishwater. Just pull the plug, and it goes down the drain. I gave the kids a tub bath without having to heat the water on the stove. When we were young, they'd never had things modern either. Mama had it worse then than I did now. At least I had electricity. REA had been acquired a couple of years before. *[Note: Actually, it was more than a couple of years before. It was when I was in grade school, because I remember when we got electricity in the one-room country school. She doesn't mention that she wired the house all by herself. She had lived in houses with electricity, and they never had enough outlets, and the outlets were in the wrong places. Furthermore, she wanted a ceiling light in every room, including the living room. So she got a book on house wiring and studied it and went to work, and we had the best-wired house in the neighborhood. The law required that the wiring be done by a licensed electrician, but the folks had a friend who was a licensed electrician, so he checked her work periodically and signed off on it. Caroline.]* Yet, right now, this seemed like the life to me.

I thought, I could just stay here. Then I knew that would never work. It was all right for awhile. But Dad wasn't so young, anymore. He was getting close to 80. He always had been harsh with us when we were kids, and he'd be much worse now. He never would be able to stand the kids. I knew I couldn't leave the older ones alone for long. A short while was all right.

Other ideas began to form in my mind. This was it. I couldn't stay here, I knew, but there was something else. The cows and sheep and horses and chickens were forgotten. Dr. Banks was right. I had too much responsibility. I would go to River City with Phil. I would at least have hot and cold running water.

I was feeling good. My depression was behind me. I was busy making plans. I wasn't the least bit concerned about the kids at home. The weather was so nice, they'd make it fine. Neither did I give it a second thought when I stepped outside, and I noticed it was getting a little colder. I went back in the house and went on dreaming about waking up in a warm room without having to start a fire with corn cobs or paper and kindling and kerosene and keep it going with coal or wood.

We went to bed that night and had a good night's sleep. The next morning, I got up, still in high spirits. I got breakfast for Dad and the kids. I again stepped outside, and the weather seemed a little colder. I thought about the kids at home. Still, what was a few degrees? Looking out the window in the forenoon, I saw a few flakes of snow. Again, what did a few flakes of snow mean the first of March? Just a little flurry, maybe. Later, I looked out the window, and the few flakes were still falling, but now they seemed different. They were swishing around. The wind was rising. I again stepped outside, and it was much colder. I thought about the kids at home. One thing, I thought, there wasn't much snow—still just a few flakes.

Nevertheless, after that, I couldn't keep from going to the window and looking out. I was ready to go home now. The wind was blowing harder, and the few flakes whipped around in swirls. The ground began to take on a glassy look, the snowflakes seeming to give it a smoother polish. I was worried now. Dad saw my constant trips to the window and tried to console me. It wouldn't amount to much. The kids would be fine. It still didn't pacify me. There was one nice thing about it. There was little snow, and Missouri was farther south than Iowa and, no doubt, was warmer. Yet, the mercury was going lower and lower.

I turned on the radio and tried to get a station in Missouri. That's when I became really worried. It was cold, and the wind was blowing there, too. What was worse, they were getting the snow Iowa wasn't. The roads were piling up in drifts. It was getting almost impossible to keep the roads cleared. Cars were piling up and stalled. I was almost frantic.

I finally called home. Phil was there. He had stayed home. While the ground was looking smoother and glassier where I was, and the still meager flakes whirled and swirled and couldn't even get a small drift from it, there was a blinding snow storm at home. I felt some better knowing Phil was home.

The next day I called again. The snow was getting no better. It was a genuine blizzard. I wanted to come home. I called the next day, and Phil was home. I asked him to come after me. "I couldn't come if I wanted to," he said. It sounded as though he didn't want to. "My car is buried halfway between here and River City. I tried to go to work. There's a 20-foot drift in front of the house. I don't know when it will get open. It's not on a mail route, so they won't get in a hurry. I can do some scooping, but that wouldn't help much."

That was that. I had to wait until he could come after me, so I took care of the kids, still more determined than ever to move to the city with Phil. I knew he would object, but that made no difference. If I had been home, he would have stayed in the city, hardly giving us a second thought, I reasoned. At least, he was getting a taste of what I had to put up with. Yet, I was anxious to get home.

After two weeks, he was able to come and get us. He acted a little peeved at me, but I didn't care. He was unable to drive the car off the main highway, so he left it there, while we trudged through half mud and ice and snow for almost a mile, carrying the two babies. When we got home, the kids met me with anger. I had left them holding the sack. They were furious, and I had no answer for them. I guessed it was rough on them, but I hadn't been expecting that kind of reception. At least they must have missed me, so I must have been good for something when I was there.

When I went back to see Dr. Banks and told him what I'd done, he seemed pleased. I told him about Phil calling me what I interpreted as an old plug work horse and that Phil had accused him of making me into a show horse. Anyway, he seemed pleased that I'd gotten up enough spunk to do something about my situation. When I told him about my reception at home, he said, "why didn't you turn around and go back up there?"

Chapter 6

Moving to the City

When I told Phil that I had decided to move to the city with him, he reacted the way I had expected him to. "The city's no place to raise kids, and besides, it would he too expensive. We could never make ends meet," he said. I guessed I'd felt the same way, and that was the reason I'd waited so long to do this. Besides giving up the livestock, I dreaded the thought of trying to raise the kids in such a crowded place.

Still, it looked as if this was the only way; I couldn't seem to take it any longer on the farm alone with the kids. Nevertheless, I didn't argue with Phil at the time. I would have to get used to the idea myself, and, besides, we couldn't move until school was out. The main thing was to get moved before school started in the fall. There really was no hurry.

Although, he didn't show much emotion on his face, I imagined Dr. Banks seemed pleased when I told him I was planning to move to the city with Phil. He asked me what I planned to do in the city.

I hadn't really given that much thought, but it dawned on me that I might have to get a job in order to keep us going. So, without giving it much thought, I told him I might get work at the State Hospital. I knew that a 46-year old woman didn't have jobs waiting for the asking, especially when they had no more education than I had. I was sure I didn't want to go out and do housework like what I had done before I was married.

There were two general hospitals in River City, but the thought struck me that working at the State Hospital wouldn't be the same as working in one of the others. Although Amelia had always said when we were growing up that she wanted to be a nurse, it had never been my desire. But I had changed some after having seven kids from when I would hold my nose with one hand and wash diapers on the board with the other when Mama had decided I needed to learn to do it. Anyway, I wasn't worrying too much about a job now. I would cross that bridge when I got to it.

Finally, one day Dr. Banks said to me, "I've started going to the State Hospital once a week to hold a clinic there the same as I hold here. If you'd rather go there, you can." I decided to do so, since I could go to Phil's apartment and maybe leave the kids.

Toby was still see-sawing back and forth, trying to decide whether he was going to quit school as soon as he reached sixteen or not. I was hoping he wouldn't quit. But the day he was sixteen, he flatly refused to go and went out and got himself a job on a farm a few miles away.

In the spring, Caroline graduated as valedictorian and got a scholarship to the state university and a chance to work for one of the deans of the school. She was to start immediately and would work eight hours a day in the summer and four hours during the school year.

Until school was out, I hadn't done too much toward getting ready to move, but when that was over, I could start out in earnest. When Phil saw I meant business about moving to the city, he tried to get a few acres near River City so we could keep a cow or two and a team and chickens and hogs, but when we started looking, we found our eighty acres would barely make a down payment on just a few acres near the city.

We decided to keep the farm and try to get a cheap house inside the city. So when Phil would find something, he would have me look at it on the days I came to see Dr. Banks.

Since we couldn't move the horses and cows inside the city limits, we had to sell them or find a place for them. I began by getting rid of the most useless animals first. Cricket, an unbroken, two-year-old sorrel filly was the first to go. Duchess, her mother, was the next one. She was a riding mare, and after my last three babies were born, I gave up even trying to ride. She was partially broken but hadn't developed any bad habits. She was almost white, with only a few scattered unnoticeable red hairs over her body and was only five years old. I priced her at $125.00, thinking it was really too cheap.

But after several men had come to look at her and hadn't bought, I decided that since she hadn't yet shed her winter coat, perhaps she didn't make such a good showing. So I came down and priced her at $100.00.

Finally, one day, a couple of men came to look at her. They wanted her, all right, but they didn't want to give what I was asking for her. They haggled and haggled, until I said, "If you want a cheaper horse, I know where there is one. Our neighbor over there on the hill has a young riding stallion they're pricing at $75."

One of the men looked up quickly and said, "I'll give $75 for her."

A sudden anger shot through me, and I snapped coldly, "Oh, no, you won't. She'll weigh 1000 pounds, and market price is 7 ½ cents. She's worth $75 on the market. If she's not worth $25 more than she'd sell on the market, I don't know why you want her in the first place."

The man smiled sheepishly, dropped his eyes and wrote me out a check for $100. Later, I heard she was being used to ride in parades and shows.

The sheep would be next, but thinking they might sell better when the ewes all had their lambs and they had a chance to get some growth on them, I took a rest from selling livestock.

The first time I went to see Dr. Banks at the State Hospital, I drove the car to Phil's apartment and left the kids there and took the bus to the hospital. I was scared. What was a state hospital like?

The three-storey red-brick building didn't look so terrible, but I knew what it was. It never dawned on me that the patients in this hospital might not be much different from the ones in the private hospital where I had taken my shock treatments.

I sat down in the large lobby, with the old-fashioned spittoons here and there and easy chairs and started to look around me. I looked beyond the wide doorway that had a sign above it that read "Mental Illness Can Be Cured" and saw a wide hallway leading straight back. It was down that hallway that Dr. Banks said he would be. I watched the doorway. I saw people in white coming and going past the doorway, so there must have been halls leading in each direction. I felt curious. Did that hall lead to the wards where patients were kept? I had never been inside a state hospital before.

I noticed there were others in the lobby with me visiting with each other. I decided some were relatives, come to see their son or mother or sister. But which one was the patient, and which one was the relative?

Then I saw some signs that read, "Open House." What was that for, I wondered? Were they having some sort of program? Yet, I saw no extra commotion. I saw nothing that might have been something going on.

In time, Dr. Banks came out of a room on down the wide hall and came to the large doorway and asked me to come with him. He shook hands and then lead me back to a large room with two desks in it. I felt a little more at home, with Dr. Banks behind the desk and me in front of it. Yet, I felt sort of funny, knowing I was in a state hospital.

I continued to come every two weeks to see him and gradually got more used to it. While riding the bus, I began to get acquainted with a woman who seemed to be on the same bus I was every time. She told me she had a son who was a patient, and she was going out to see him. I saw them visiting while I waited in the lobby for my doctor, and I noticed her son seemed terribly nervous. It seemed as if he was expecting a bear or lion to jump out from behind a door.

As the weeks went by, I felt more and more relaxed. Dr. Banks began to seem more like a friend instead of Sherlock Holmes. He showed his pleasure, I thought, in my improvement, as he asked me every so often if I had applied for work at the hospital. I'd have to tell him I hadn't. I had lost my nerve. Was it what I wanted to do, anyway? I finally told him I didn't think I could do the work. He insisted I could do it as well as anyone else could. It was still scary.

Once he told me I should be working with people instead of animals, that I was wasting my talent. I couldn't see it. I was scared of people unless I could feel lost in a crowd, or else I could sit and talk to a single person. I was sure I had no talent for working with people.

One day, I saw a mischievous gleam come into the doctor's eyes, as he started reaching toward a pile of brown folders. What was he up to, I wondered. He picked out one of the folders and shoved it toward me. On the outside was something written. It was my folder, and the words I read said something about a desert flower being too far away to be enjoyed, or something like that.

Immediately I knew what it meant, and, feeling embarrassed, I pushed it back to him. Again, he was telling me I had talent. I knew he was proud of me.

A few minutes after I had shoved it back, a feeling of curiosity came over me. I had read his personal opinion of me on the outside, but what was the medical opinion on the inside? Why had I given it back to him when I held it in my hands? Why hadn't I opened it up and read the inside?

"Let me read the inside," I blurted out with a little bit of teasing, not really expecting him to oblige. If he could tease, why couldn't I?

He gave me one of his long searching stares, and then, to my surprise, he got the folder and gave it to me again. Unsure of myself now, I turned to the page that said diagnosis.

I began to read and then felt stunned. It said mine was a neurosis, but that a psychosis was imminent. I wasn't sure of the exact meaning of the word, imminent, but whatever it meant, I was sure it wasn't good. Did it mean possible or probable? Somehow, just reading it gave me a scare. Still, that was all past. That had been about two years before.

I then read about my IQ. There were several numbers—105, 120, 116—and, to my surprise, I was the lowest in numbers. Algebra, geometry and math had been my best subjects in school. I had been good in reading in the elementary grades, although the books I'd had to read had been few. I said something to him about that 105 in numbers and told him those had been my best subjects. He said, "That's different." I wondered how it was different.

I read that I was paranoid and wasn't too surprised about that. I guessed I was kind of suspicious at times. I was perplexed, however, when I read that Dad was mean or something like that and that Mama was all right but ineffective or something similar. Surely, I hadn't said that in my autobiography. Then I remembered that this had, no doubt, been written before I had written my autobiography. It came from the tests I had taken.

Dad had been stern and maybe had some old-country old-fashioned ideas about women's place in the home, like the women worked and minded the men, but I had never thought of him as mean. We had been terribly poor, and he had been so busy trying to make a living for a big family, perhaps he had never had the time for the kids. He was terribly tense and a floor-pacer and a worrier. I always thought I had taken my temperament from him.

Mama was different, however. She would get all excited about things and would get upset at the time, but she would get over things, while Dad would stew and worry for weeks at a time. He was a deep thinker, I was sure, and I could remember seeing him staring into space, as though his mind was a million miles away.

I was sure that Mama had been an extremely strong woman, even though she was sort of flighty. She had high ideals, I thought. She believed men should be the boss or, at least, the head of the house. Anyway, that was the idea I had gotten from her.

I continued to read. It seemed I had a very poor prognosis. I was given a 50-50 chance of coming out of it, but, because of my high IQ, with ECT, I might get better. I still doubted the ECT had helped me.

The first thing I did when I got home was to look up the word imminent. It meant what I'd been afraid it meant—probable and soon. Still, that was all past, and I needn't worry about it now.

Finally, Phil found a house in town, and on the last of May we signed the papers. It was a cheap one—a basement house, with five rooms and no bath, except for the stool under the stairway. I still had to take a bath in the old galvanized wash tub. There was, however, hot and cold running water, so I didn't have to pump and carry my water. With gas heat, neither would I have to build fires with wood and coal. It wasn't exactly a prize, but, at least, it was on a bus route, in case I got some work. Four railroad lines were just a block away and the big Quaker Oats plant was just on the other side, so it was a noisy part of the city.

One day, while we were signing the papers on the house, I got to talking to a man who said his wife had worked at the

State Hospital. He said it wasn't so bad and encouraged me to apply. I did, but I would have to come back another day to take the test the state gave. When I told Dr. Banks that I had finally applied, I knew it pleased him.

In the meantime, I had gotten around to trying to sell my sheep. A man who claimed he was an expert on sheep came from quite a distance to look at them. They weren't in the lot, but since he would want to get a closer look at them, we had to get them lotted. The expert began to give us all orders where to stand and everything. He seemed to be a man who expected to give orders and have everyone follow them.

But with the kids and me all placed in his strategic positions, it wasn't long before my pets were running in every direction like wild jackrabbits. I guessed my sheep didn't like sheep experts. Anyway, we were only able to get about two sheep lotted, and, of course, he didn't buy the sheep.

A few days later, another man, who claimed to know very little about sheep, came to look at them. It so happened that the sheep were out in the pasture, and we had to walk out to where they were. While we stood and talked, the sheep paid little attention to us. I would walk up to one and put my arms around her, and the man would look in her mouth.

Little Iodine (They were all named after comic strip characters, after the first few that the boys wanted to give names like Carburetor and Magneto and Crankshaft) was one of the originals that Phil had lugged home from the stockyards ten years before. The man was surprised that she was that old and said, "That's the first ten-year-old ewe I've seen with a tooth."

While my sheep stood or lay in the shade, placidly chewing their cuds, we haggled over the price. After some time of this haggling, I took off some from my price, and the man agreed to take them. He would be back in a few days, he said, to pick them up.

I had no really good place for loading, and, remembering the mess we'd had the other time, I said to the two men, "You men stand around nearby and pay no attention to the sheep. Pretend you're fixing fence or something and have no interest in the sheep. I'll get them in the truck, and then you can come up and put down the end-gate."

Even though they might have believed I was crazy, they did as I told them to do. While the men tinkered around, I started to call them, "Come on. Come on." Little Iodine put her head in the air and started to follow me, while I began walking slowly toward the truck. One by one the others followed her. The lambs came next, and the old buck came last. He wasn't a pet; he was just following his girls.

I walked up the ramp and into the truck with the sheep right after me. When we were all in the truck, the men walked up quietly and locked us in. I clambered over the front end and down to the ground, leaving 20 ewes, 20 lambs and a buck in the truck. The trucker walked toward the cab, laughing, and said, "That was the easiest bunch of sheep I've ever loaded. Next time I have a load, I'm coming after you."

Still, with determination, I watched a little sadly as the truck lumbered down the road with my sheep in it.

Finally, I went to River City and took the test. When I walked into the State Employment Agency and saw dozens of men and women filling out papers, I felt rather discouraged. I won't have a chance, I thought, with that many applications. But when the ones taking the test for attendant were called, only a few got up and went into the small room. I realized, now, that there might be lots of state jobs besides state hospital jobs.

But when I started on the tests and found I was having trouble seeing the small print, I felt scared. I had known for some time I was getting more and more far-sighted, but so far, I had solved the problem by holding my reading matter farther from my face. It didn't work here. I began to get nervous and worry when I saw some finish and leave the room. It didn't seem so hard, but would I ever get done? There was a time limit. Would I fail because of that? I was one of the last to finish.

When I told Dr. Banks about my having taken the test for attendant, he assured me he was sure I would get on in time, although there was some red tape about it. I felt no such optimism. Anyway, I wouldn't get my grades back for a couple of weeks and could forget it for the time being.

Again, I started feeling guilty about taking up Dr. Banks' time and suggested I quit. I realized I felt a tinge of fear about throwing away my crutch, but I knew I'd have to stop seeing him sometime.

This time he agreed I was ready and said, "I'm going to Europe for about six weeks, anyway, and you can't see me. But when I get back around the first of September, I'd like to see you once more to see how you're getting along. By that time, you'll be moved and probably be working."

So, I went home to do some more getting ready to move and sell some more livestock. I had been selling my cows off, one at a time, as they freshened. With a new calf by her side and a large udder and a smooth glistening Guernsey hide, she was at her best for selling. I had several two-year-olds having their first calf. It hurt me to see them go, the same as I dreaded to think of having to give up Babe and Jean, my faithful Belgian work team.

I didn't have to advertise Babe and Jean for sale. For several years, every so often, some horse trader would stop by and try to get them away from me. It wouldn't be long, I knew, before one would be around. It was sickening just to think of this giant exodus of the draft horse off the farms and into tin cans. But what could I do? The fences weren't good enough to leave them on the farm and move 50 miles away. Besides, we needed the money. There were few draft horses left on the farms, and mine were among the last.

Horses had always been my love. I had been slow to talk, but mama used to tell me my first words were, "I wish I had a pony." I couldn't call Babe and Jean ponies, but they were horses. Now, cows were cows, and hogs were hogs, and I liked them all, but horses were something else. They were almost people. I had felt confident that Duchess and Cricket had not gone into cans. But for my work team, I had to put blinders on my conscience.

It didn't help that I sold them for twice the amount I'd given for them eight years before after working them for eight years. Besides, Jean was about eighteen years old and Babe only a couple of years younger. They were getting to be old horses.

The morning the truck was to come after my team, I went to the field to get them and found the two mares at the far end of the farm in the center of a grove of small slender trees. I stopped at the edge of the grove. The whole floor of the grove was covered with a mat of the most vicious-looking three-leafed plant with those unmistakable blisters on the leaves. It was shady, and I could understand the team's choosing it for a resting place.

I went no further and started calling the horses. Jean was standing and just gave me a look with her warm horse-eyes. If Babe came toward me, she would have followed, but Babe was not standing, and she was too lazy to get up on her feet. I called and called, but neither mare made a move to come. Both just gave me an unconcerned look.

What should I do? I didn't really want to sell them, and maybe they didn't want to be sold. Yet, that's what I had come to do. I knew what Dr. Banks would say if I got the itch. Nevertheless, I had to have them up to the house. Finally, I gave up and tip-toed through the rich carpet of ivy, hoping I could keep from touching any of it, which was unlikely. I'd had my shots, but I wasn't sure they were infallible.

So, with two lead ropes in my hand and Babe on one side and Jean on the other, I headed for the house. Thoughts of Dr. Banks' sarcasm flashed across my mind if I contracted the allergy. Fury began to rise inside me, and I began to rave. He had no right to accuse me of getting poison ivy deliberately. He was downright ridiculous. I raved on. The horses, with thoughts of shooing away the flies, switched their tails and shook their heads and rattled their halters and ignored my anger. I got madder and madder, perhaps taking away some of the sting of giving up the horses. Yet, it was with a heavy heart that I watched the horses go. The old gray mare, she ain't what she usta be, I thought. Going, going and gone was the plight of the draft horse. It was a sad day, and nothing could stop it. This was progress.

By this time, two weeks had passed since I had taken my test, and it was about time for the returns to come. I began to watch the mail with anxiety. Had I passed? How could I have passed? How could I have failed? Finally they came, and I'd passed with a grade of 88, and with the grades came a letter telling me to report to the personnel manager at the State Hospital to be interviewed.

This time, I rode the bus and got off at a building much different from the one where I had been seeing Dr. Banks. The wide circling driveways and the lush green grass and scattered elm and cottonwood and cedar and maple and pine of the surrounding grounds gave the place a park-like atmosphere. The four-storey gray-white brick building with wings spreading toward the back made me think of a great white bird ready to take off in flight. The tall slender windows with rounded tops and bars on them almost gave it the appearance of a castle. To me, however, with my fear of insanity all my life, it seemed to have a sinister look to it.

As I walked up the wide front steps and onto the large porch, fear gripped me. Inside the large lobby with a wide stairway before me, I sensed a quiet dignity. It was hard for me to believe I was inside a state hospital.

I was directed into a room and was interviewed by the personnel manager, Mr. Wright, who was really a pleasant-looking round-faced man, but at the time, seemed like an ogre to me. He asked me questions, and I answered them, while I was almost afraid to breath. He didn't ask me if I'd had ECT, and I didn't tell him. But when he asked me why I thought I would like to work at this hospital, I answered, "I don't know that I will like to work here. I'll have to work here first before I'll know."

After I'd said it, I was stunned at my answer. What a crazy thing to say. Now, I'll never get the job for sure. I had flubbed that time. When he finished with me, he said, "If you are picked, you'll get a letter in about two weeks to report for work. If not, it'll probably three or four months before you will be called."

I went home to wait some more and to finish my moving. Phil had moved into our new house, and we had been moving a few things at a time in the pickup. We had sold all our cattle except one, and Phil's sister had agreed to take her for the milk and half of the calf at butchering time. We still had hopes of finding a few acres near the city where we could keep a cow.

We decided to keep the hogs for awhile, since we had the corn to feed them, and they weren't ready for market. We could also butcher a couple when it got colder. We'd come out two or three times a week to throw out feed for them and fill up their water troughs.

When two weeks had passed, and I had received no letter from the state to report for work, I began to get discouraged. After another week or two, I gave up. It was almost time for school to start, and we would have to be moved. So, one day, while reading the ads in the daily newspaper, I saw one from one of the other hospitals advertising for nurse's aides.

I applied for that job, and all I had to do was to fill out an application and talk to a woman, without taking a test or a physical or anything. They could put me right to work, she told me, on the 7 to 3:30 shift. But I wanted the night shift so I could care for Cynthia and Edward in the daytime. She told me then that they had nothing on that shift at the present, but she was sure there would be an opening in a few days. So I waited.

We didn't know what to do with the old gray gander. He was too old and tough to roast, and we couldn't give him away. His mate had died a few years before, and since that time, he had ranged with the cows or sheep. So now he would have to be a hog and run with the hogs. It seemed that geese are social animals.

The day we moved, Phil loaded Smokey and her calf into the pickup and took her to his sister's farm.

Chapter 7

Adjusting to City Life and Getting a Job

We got moved, and right away the hospital called and said they had an opening on the 11 to 7 shift. Although I could start immediately, I would have to work two weeks on orientation on the 7 to 3:30 shift. I had to hunt up a temporary baby-sitter for those two weeks. Phil found a woman who was taking care of a couple of her grandchildren at the time, and it would be easy for her to care for mine at the same time.

I was scared that first day as I went to the information window to get my orders, and the training nurse, Mrs. Murphy, arrived and took me to the ground floor, where she explained the time clock to me. It looked complicated; I had never punched one before. Then she took me on the elevator to the top floor and left me on the pediatric ward, which was where I was to work on the night shift.

Several nurses were at the desk in the nurses station, which was sandwiched between two rooms with large windows, where the babies could be seen without going inside the room. Some were standing; some were sitting.

The nurses paid little attention to me, and I was turned over to a small nurse's aide in a blue uniform like mine. While passing out the stainless steel wash basins to the various rooms, she took me with her, giving me some instructions as she went. Later, we returned to the rooms and collected the basins, and about 8 o'clock a large food wagon, filled with trays of food with name cards on them, arrived. I felt like a dunce as the small aide told me just where to send the trays. She must have hated this job of breaking in a new aide.

Later, we picked up the empty trays and placed them back on the food cart. When it was rolled outside the ward, I was surprised when we again deposited the basins, along with clean towels and wash cloths. This, I learned, was for their morning baths.

About that time, Mrs. Murphy returned and took me on a tour of the hospital. We went from one floor to another, stopping at OB and the lab and every place. I would have to go to OB every night to pick up the formulas, and in the mornings, I would have to deposit the specimens I had collected during the night. I felt as if I were spinning in circles. Directions had no meaning for me whatsoever.

She showed me where the kitchen was and the cafeteria and a room where I was to poke certain papers under the door at night when everything was locked up. She took me to the basement, a scary place, where I would have to go after ice for the oxygen tents and drinking water.

How, I wondered, will I ever remember all this when I couldn't tell when I turned left or I turned right? East was west, and north was south, and up was down, as far as I was concerned. But Mrs. Murphy was nice and said, "I know you'll never remember all this, but as you get used to it, everything will come to you."

She took me back to pediatrics and left again with the little nurse's aide to teach me some more. The aide showed me how to make a hospital bed and how to miter the corners and all.

It wasn't long, however, before Mrs. Murphy was back for some more training. She also showed me how to make a hospital bed and then a post-operative bed. She taught me how to set up an oxygen tent, which was nothing but a jumble in my head. She explained the workings of the oxygen bottles and where to put the ice. I was whisked back and forth from the aide to Mrs. Murphy.

The aides had a hide-away, in behind the utility room, where they could go and get out of sight when their work was done, and where the nurses knew where they were and could find them if they needed them. We were supposed to sew and patch things for the hospital. The nurses seldom came back there, except for one nice nurse, who would come and visit with us every so often. I'd heard she was leaving soon to go to the State Hospital.

One day, she told me about the night nurse I would be working with and said, "She can be cranky at times, but don't let it worry you. When you get to know her, she can be lots of fun."

After I had worked a week on orientation, Mrs. Murphy told me they were dispensing with one week and I was to go on nights right away. I had heard that the night aide whose place I was taking had gotten ulcers and was having to change to days. It should have been a warning to me, but I didn't heed it. I knew night would bother me at first, but I was sure I would soon get adjusted.

It was also time for Dr. Banks to return from his trip, and I was to go and see him for the last time. He appeared pleased I had gotten a job, although I had the feeling he would still like for me to get on at the State Hospital. He said, "I'm sure you'll get on there in time. It takes several months in a place like that."

When my time was up, Dr. Banks shook hands and said, "If you feel that you need me at any time, call and have them set up an appointment for you." I left feeling the separation not too keenly. My crutch was no farther away than the telephone.

Our new home, I soon learned, had its problems. To the north of us were several vacant lots, with a high hill where kids could climb and dig tunnels and caves, which could be dangerous. Besides, along one side of the lots lived an old lady with a boy friend who seemed to hate kids unless they were the kind that sat and acted like old people. My kids weren't that kind, and neither were the boys next door toward the south.

The boys were twins and were about a year older than Cynthia. They were so fascinated with their new neighbors and were under our feet constantly while we were moving. All we had to do was to turn around and they were there, watching us with wide-open eyes. Besides those two boys, there was another set of twin boys a year older than they were a few houses down the street. There was also a set of ten-year-old girls within the block. There were dozens of other kids living in the six houses down the street within the block. Only about ten feet separated each house.

I remembered the nice nurse's words when I came to work that first night after the afternoon nurses had left. Mrs. Wallace, the colored nurse who was to be my boss from now on, was really put out when she learned I hadn't stopped at the kitchen and brought up the jar of coffee which the little crippled lady who cleaned up late at night had prepared for us. In the first place, I thought, I hadn't been told about it. How did she expect me to know? Anyway, she sent me back after it.

When I entered the kitchen, which was located on the ground floor, and saw on the counter before me rows of jars of various shapes and sizes and colors filled with coffee, I hesitated to take one. I saw no one around. Then I saw a small crippled woman come into sight from between refrigerators and stoves and come toward me. When I reached for a jar, she began to rave at me for getting the wrong jar. I stepped back and felt as if someone had beat me with an iron rod. With anger written all over her face, she told me which one was mine. I hugged my jar and hurried back to the elevator and rode to the fifth floor. I was getting initiated that first night.

As soon as Mrs. Wallace and I were alone, she got the flashlight and told me to go with her. We went into every room, and she checked the names on the beds of the new patients and the other information. I just followed and watched her.

When we were finished with that and had returned to the nurse's station, she began to tell me what my duties were. I listened and wasn't sure I would ever remember it all. One of the first things I was to do was to check the new patients' ages and everything to learn from which ones I could get the urine specimens without making a special container out of adhesive tape and test tubes.

But when she tried to teach me how to make those containers from test tubes, and I didn't get the hang of it right off, she didn't like it, I knew. Besides, she didn't act very friendly, even though I tried to do my best. Somehow, she wasn't liking me, I thought.

She acted a little stand-offish the second night, and also the third night. Then she said, irritably, "I get one aide broken in, and then they send me another one, and I have to teach her all over again."

So that was it. She didn't like to teach new aides. But that's a little unreasonable, I reasoned to myself. What did she expect? No one should quit?

Every night before I went to my ward on the top floor, I'd stop at the kitchen to pick up my jar of coffee. But each time, I was unable to remember for certain which was mine, and sure as anything, she'd jump down my throat, as if I had committed a major crime for not knowing. It wasn't easy, because some were identified by where they sat on the table only, and some were so similar. There were square jars and round jars and triangle jars and pint jars and quart jars and green jars and clear jars. Some were filled nearer the top than others. I dreaded the entrance into her den.

I soon learned I wasn't alone in my fear of the little woman. The other aides also hated the job. Some would peek through the door and make a dive for a jar when they saw her not looking, making her madder than ever when she came in and her jar wasn't there. Some flatly refused to go, saying that if the nurse wanted her coffee, let her go after it herself. The aide said she would rather do without. I didn't have that much nerve.

Finally, after batting the problem around in my head for several days, I hit on an idea. I would have something nice to say to her on the tip of my tongue just as I entered and say it before she had a chance to say anything, and she would have to answer me. It worked.

After a few times of this, I'd see her look up with a scowl on her face as I came through the door, evidently on the verge of giving someone a good bawling out. But when she saw it was me, her face would soften, and she wouldn't say it. In time she would sneak us a little bit extra, like a cup of ice cream, for our ward. People, I thought, could be like animals; it worked to use psychology on them.

Gradually, as I learned more about how to do things, the nurse came out of her shell, and we had some interesting times.

I would tell her stories about the farm, which she knew nothing about, and she would laugh hysterically. I was the funniest thing she ever saw, she would tell me.

She wondered why she couldn't buy mountain oysters in stores like steak or bacon or ham. I told her it was because most male animals were castrated before they ever reached the market. Farmers ate them themselves or just threw them away.

That got her. She thought each cow had to have her own bull and each hen had her own rooster. When she got a farm, she said, she was going to make sure every female had her own mate. I kind of thought she was some funny. One day, I brought her some mountain oysters Phil had gotten at the stockyards.

Every so often we'd go to the farm to throw out corn to the hogs and see that they had water until we would return. The old gray gander was always there to meet us with his neck stretched skyward and honking a loud welcome. He was like an old grandmother on Thanksgiving Day with the arrival of all the family. I felt sorry for the old bird.

I was learning more and more about my work all the time, but as the weeks passed, I found out it wasn't as easy to get adjusted to the night work as I had believed it would be. Getting the proper sleep in the day time wasn't easy. I tried to snatch sleep while the babies slept and after the others got home from work or school. It was such a broken sleep.

Besides, I had salesmen and insurance men knocking on my door any time of the day. The milkman delivered the milk without waking me, but he did have to collect. I did try to train the regular collectors, but if there was a change, I'd have it to do all over again.

I started missing my milk and cream and orange juice, but the milkman insisted he'd left it. Then one day I heard a noise outside and opened the door just in time to see two small pre-school boys running with their arms loaded with cartons of orange juice and milk.

I took after them, as one carton dropped on the ground, and the mother came outside and was there to meet us. She said she had some more orange juice in her refrigerator she had taken away from them when she had found them in the back yard drinking it. But she didn't know where it had come from.

Another time, the little guy was in my front yard bothering things, so I told him to go home. He faced me defiantly and told me he didn't have to; this was his property, and he was going to stay. I picked up a switch that had fallen off a tree and held it in my hands with no intention of using it. He reached down and picked up a twig, maybe about six inches long, and stood there facing me bravely, like Samson facing Goliath.

My own kids were a little mixed up, too. One day, they became determined to go out and see the cow in the milk truck.

My old yellow cat was having her problems as well as the rest of us. Our dog had died before we came to the city, but we did have our old pussy cat. On the farm, she had been a well-adjusted mouser and could catch three mice or rats in one pounce—one in her mouth and one under each paw.

But in the city she became a clinging hysterical coward, sinking her sharp claws into our flesh if we tried to put her outside, where she could hear the cars whirring by and the trucks on the main stockyards route into town about a block away and the trains clanging and roaring and whistling on the other side of the street and the noisy Quaker Oats plant just beyond it going 24 hours a day. She was a maniac, if there ever was one.

But as the weeks went by, she became braver and would sit on the stone wall surrounding the yard. The neighbors said, when they saw the cat, "You won't have a cat very long. That little dog across the street won't let her stay. He drives every cat away. He owns this street."

"I'll bet on the old cat," I said. I couldn't picture any dog getting the best of her.

Sure enough, when the little dog spied the cat, he flew to our side of the street. A minute later, the dog was yelping back across the street. But the dog wasn't whipped. Undaunted, the dog returned, but in a matter of seconds, he was again yelping back to his side, with his tail tucked between his legs, and the cat turned and let him go in peace. She wasn't asking for trouble, but she wouldn't back off from it.

It happened the third time, with the same results. From then on, the old cat sat on the stone wall, calmly washing her face, seemingly unaware of the small dog across the street eyeing her longingly but too scared to follow up his urges.

Soon after having come to the city, I learned the late night busses had a different atmosphere about them with fewer riders than the crowded middle of the day busses. The regular bus driver was a friendly man and there was a friendly bantering and kidding between the riders and the driver.

Usually, the same riders rode every night. One elderly retired man was always kidding the middle-aged driver, who must have been a widower, about getting him a wife. Seeing my blue uniform and knowing I was an aide at the hospital, he soon brought me into it and asked me to find him one among the other aides. I began to get in with the spirit and started to kid the aides who weren't married about finding a wife for the bus driver. I was enjoying myself.

An entirely different mood pervaded the early morning bus I had to ride home. While I was having a rough time trying to stay awake so as not to miss my getting off place, the others were quietly reading their morning paper, looking fresh and ready to go.

I had almost forgotten about the State Hospital, when about two months after starting work at the hospital, I received a letter from the state to report for work and to take my physical. I felt some excitement. I was getting $115 a month and worked six days a week, but the State Hospital was paying $178 a month, and they only worked five days a week. I thought about that extra $63 and what I could do with it. It was tempting all right, but my second thoughts were about the type of patients I would be caring for. Fear hit me. I had this job. I could do this.

Could I do the other? Fear won out over greed and I ignored the letter. That was the end of that, I thought.

I continued to work where I was. The nights could be terribly long at times. One night we might have six patients; the next night it might be twice that many, or even more. It was the nights we had the least work that were the longest. I'd go to the serving room and scour the already shining and spotless stainless steel sink and counter tops over and over to try to stay awake. It simply wasn't easy to turn nights into days. I would get so sleepy I'd get sick at my stomach and could hardly walk the two blocks in the morning to meet the bus.

Some of the aides told me they didn't envy me my ward. They wouldn't want pediatrics for anything. I felt that if I'd had my choice, this would have been the one I would have picked. It was more interesting, I imagined, than some of the others. In the daytime, the nurses mostly took care of the small babies, and especially the incubator babies. But at night, with only the nurse and myself there, I got to help the nurse take care of these babies, and even the incubator babies.

One thing that bothered me, however, were the two-year-old children having their legs straightened who had to wear those casts. The post-polio, also, bothered me, because it seemed they did so much whimpering. Having the mothers and fathers around, I thought, was one reason the other aides didn't like that ward. They didn't bother me, though.

One night, when coming on the ward, I saw a well-dressed elderly distinguished-looking man standing at the nurses' station, giving orders right and left. It's a doctor, I thought, although I'd never seen him before, but there were lots of doctors I never got to see, working the hours I did. Anyway, he certainly was wanting to have his patient cared for right.

After he left, I was surprised to learn that he was only an attendant at the State Hospital. He had seemed to know—or acted like he knew—so much about everything. I was also surprised to learn he had a small baby in the hospital. Grandchild might have seemed more reasonable.

Then I went into the room where his baby was to get the baby prepared to take the urine specimen. I was surprised, again, when I saw the mother of the baby, the old man's wife. She was about as pretty and attractive a young woman, perhaps in her early 20's, that you could find. How come, I wondered, didn't she go after a younger man. Surely, with her looks, she could have gotten one.

I had trouble getting the tape to stick on the baby, until I told the mother not to powder the little girl. I was in the room quite some time, and the young woman was very friendly and talkative. I learned she had worked as an attendant, herself, although at the time she wasn't. I was interested and listened closely. She didn't make it sound bad at all. I began to wish I'd gone out and had taken the physical. But that was past. my chance was gone, I thought.

For a short time after I'd moved to the city, things at home went along fairly smoothly. But as the weeks went by, it seemed that Phil and I were having trouble adjusting. I tried to talk things over with him, but, as usual, he appeared to think there was nothing to talk over. I was wrong, and he was right, and that was that. He simply couldn't communicate. I tried to get him to go with me to the Family Guidance and get some marriage counseling, but again, he seemed to think it was useless. His attitude was that if I'd change, everything would be all right. They couldn't do anything.

Finally, I went on my own, but the counselor insisted that Phil come also. Phil still refused to go. My counselor continued to urge me to get Phil to go, until Phil did go a time or two. It turned out it wasn't as bad as he had imagined it would be. We went at different times, and I imagined it did help some. But Phil didn't keep on going, partly because his hours at work made it a little unhandy.

I kept on going, however, since the Family Guidance counselor thought I needed a little therapy to keep up my confidence in my work. I couldn't avert that feeling of being a failure and the "I can't" from coming over me. When he quit to take a better job, he turned me over to another worker.

In November, about a month after I'd gotten the first letter from the state telling me to report at the State Hospital for a physical, I received another letter telling me the same thing. I, again, felt frightened. I wanted the job. I wanted that extra money and that extra day off. Even with the $10 raise I was eligible to receive this next month where I was, I would still be getting $53 more money at the State Hospital.

Then I'd think about the kind of hospital it was. During some of my conversations about the work there, I'd heard it said that attendants could be left alone with as many as 60 or 100 patients. Were they exaggerating? I couldn't be sure. Those patients might be dangerous. But why would they say it if it weren't so?

Then I remembered that young mother who had worked there, and she made it sound interesting. I weighed and measured the pros and the cons. Fifty three dollars wasn't chicken feed. Finally, this time, greed triumphed over fear, and I decided in favor of the money.

So, in the daytime, when I should have been sleeping, I went to the State Hospital, and again got off the bus at that long gray-white building that looked so imposing.

Almost paralyzed with fear, I walked up those front steps and entered the lobby and went to the information desk. This time, a pleasant-looking woman, who I learned later was one of the supervisors, came and talked to me. She was very nice, and when she saw I was scared, she assured me there was nothing to be afraid of and said she had also been scared when she started.

First, she started to tell me how to get to the building where I would take my physical and then decided she would take me over there herself. We wound around and between buildings and up walks and across lawns until we stood before another red-brick building that looked something like the building where I'd had my conferences with Dr. Banks. Inside I faced a long tunnel sloping downward with an opening at the other end. I had the sensation I was looking through the wrong end of a telescope at my feet. It looked spooky and mysterious.

She left me in a room just around the corner. Although it didn't have the spic-and-span look the lab in the other hospital had, it was definitely that. Two other women were waiting. After getting our urine specimens, they first got the blood sample from the one and then tried the other woman, but they had trouble there.

They tried one arm, but never got a drop; they tried the other. Still, there was nothing there. After jabbing around on it, they tried the wrist with the same results. They tried the other wrist, moving the needle around. I watched, mesmerized, unable to turn my eyes away. They jabbed and jabbed and changed spots some more, until they finally had just a few drops. Squinting at the test tube one said, "Maybe we can make this do if we're careful." I was entranced.

As she tied the tourniquet around my arm, the woman said happily, "This is the way we like them."

We were sent upstairs on the elevator, where a couple of nurses sat at a desk in the hall. We were told to sit on the chairs along the hall wall and wait. We waited and waited while the nurses talked and wrote and talked on the telephone from time to time. No one really seemed too busy. An attendant went into rooms and talked to the nurses, while the nurses mostly just sat. Another woman, dressed in a print dress, wearing anklets, also seemed to be trying to work, but she was doing more talking than anything else. A patient, no doubt.

I began to get nervous and restless. I was sleepy. Where was the doctor? I watched the nurses and waited. It seemed I'd been sitting there an hour.

At one point, I became fascinated with the conversation of one of the nurses on the telephone.

"No, Doctor, we have no room for him," she was saying, "But we have no room. We can't move anyone. There is no place where we can put him. No, Doctor, we can't take him. We can't."

Over and over, the nurse insisted there was no room for the man. She finally hung up, and in a few minutes, as if the man had been outside the door, a cart was rolled through the door with a wasted away man, with no color in his face at all. He was pushed on down the hall.

I started waiting again. After what seemed like an hour, one of the women was told to go inside a room. Now, I thought, it won't be long. It can't take the doctor long to examine her. I was mistaken. She must have been in there at least a half hour. She came out, and I thought, now, it won't be long. Again, I was mistaken. At least another half hour passed before the other woman was told to go inside. The same thing happened again. I waited and waited, getting more and more tired and nervous. When she came out, I thought, this is it. Surely, they'll take me soon. I must have waited another half hour and then I was finally told to go in the room.

The nurse told me to take off every stitch of clothing. I lay down on a table, and she covered me with a sheet. It will soon be over, I thought. I could see inside an adjacent room where two men were talking. One was dark-skinned, and from the words of conversation I could overhear, he had a strong foreign accent. The other man had a light skin and had no accent.

Which is the doctor? Surely one of them must be. Enough words came through to me that I got it the one man was trying to convert the dark-skinned man to the Christian religion. I waited while they talked, apparently oblivious of my existence. What was this, I wondered. They talked and talked and talked. I was feeling disgusted, but what could I do now? I was here, and I was being given no consideration at all. My time was worth nothing. The other hospital hadn't even given me a physical.

The doctor finally did come in and examine me and asked me at one point, "How long have you had these lumps in your breast?"

I was stunned and scared and said, "I didn't know I had any."

He laughed and said, "Oh, don't get excited. There's nothing there."

When I left for home that day, I wasn't feeling very enthusiastic about the State Hospital. I was afraid that I might be making a mistake. It would take about three days for them to know if I passed the physical. I should call out there and find out.

I didn't tell the other hospital when I went to work what I'd done. I might not pass. I'll wait until I find out, I thought. After three days, I called the State Hospital as soon as I got off work in the morning. I called from a pay telephone at the hospital.

The woman said I had passed, and they wanted me to report for work Monday morning.

"No," I said. "I haven't told this hospital about it, and I want to give them two weeks notice."

"We want you right away," she said.

"I don't think it's any more than right to give them that much notice. Unless they release me, I won't come."

She was insistent, but I was just as insistent. Finally, she said, "All right. We would like to be treated the same way if it were turned around."

Leaving the phone booth, I went to the personnel office and gave them the notice. I told them the State Hospital wanted me right away, but I would stay two weeks to give them a chance to get someone to replace me.

Chapter 8

Starting Work
at the State Hospital

I was surprised when the hospital called me at home and told me that they had found someone to take my place and I could quit immediately, so I called the State Hospital and told them I could start right away.

It was November 23, 1959, just a few months over two years after being a patient in a private psychological hospital and having taken nine shock treatments, that I started work at the River City State Hospital as an attendant. I stepped from the city bus that morning about 8 a.m., wearing my blue nurse's aide uniform, since I hadn't had a chance to buy a white one.

I was plenty scared, all right. Had I made a mistake to change jobs? What was in store for me? This job paid more money, but how did I know I could do it? I'd been making out on the other one, but if this didn't pan out, I might be out of a job. Maybe I felt just a little guilty for having evaded the fact that I'd had ECT. Dr. Banks had believed in my ability to do the work, but could I?

Half in terror and half in expectancy, I walked up those front steps for the third time. But this was the real thing. I would know what it would be like before long.

So, with shaky legs and a sinking feeling in my stomach, I asked directions at the information desk. Following her explanation, I walked up the wide stairway in the center of the lobby and, turning at the top, walked toward the rear until I came to a large room with filing cabinets in it. On one side was another room connected with a large doorway. It must have been the personnel office. Soon, a woman came from the room and told me to take a chair and wait for Mr. Wright.

Soon, two young women came and also took chairs. Then, an older woman, perhaps a little older than I was, came. At first, there was an awkward silence in the room until someone started talking. It seemed that I wasn't the only one who felt anxiety. But as we talked, I thought, they didn't have as much reason as I had. The two young women, I learned, were sisters, and they already had a sister working here. The older woman had been working in the state hospital in another state for 10 years as a psychiatric aide.

After some time, Mr. Wright came, and, after collecting some papers and material, he told us to follow him. He led us down the hall and up some narrow steps and down another narrow hallway, as we passed closed doors, until we finally reached a door and went inside. It was a long narrow room with a large window at the far end. It was covered by heavy drapes, and the blinds were closed, so it seemed dark inside. I was still apprehensive.

A long table was in the center of the room with plenty of chairs around it. Mr. Wright took the chair at the head of the table, and we took chairs along the sides. I now felt weak and shaky. By this time I was sure I'd made a mistake. This room even made me feel as if I were locked in a turret in some mysterious castle. Mr. Wright had turned on the lights, but it still seemed dark.

Mr. Wright began to talk after he had given each of us a couple of booklets, explaining that the one on The Rules and Regulations of the Merit System did not belong to us, and if for any reason we quit working there, we were to return it to the Hospital. The other booklet was on the Retirement Plan. He explained that 4% of our wages would be withheld to go into this fund, but if we quit before retirement age, it would be returned to us.

He then explained about the Merit System. It had such a high-sounding name that I thought it must be all right, but as he talked, I felt somewhat confused. I tried my best to get everything he was saying, but some of it was confusing. What if I don't understand some of it? My anxiety, no doubt, was mixing me up more than ever.

When I heard him say something about the union, I became frightened. "I'm required to tell you there is a union here," he was saying, "but you don't have to join. It's up to you. You won't get fired if you do join, and no one can make you join."

Years before, Phil had started to work where there was a union. I had thought unions were something terrible, but since that time I'd changed. Nevertheless, this was the first time I'd had the choice of joining. My anxiety was growing.

He continued, "The union here is terribly weak. It has no power, and, anyway, the Merit System takes the place of the union. It does everything the union can do, and it does it better."

He had said we wouldn't get fired if we joined, but I wasn't sure. I had the feeling he would rather we didn't join. Now I felt conflict. Should I join, or shouldn't I?

He took us downstairs to the lobby, and, after looking around to find someone who would show us where to go, he said, "I'll take you over there myself. I have to go, anyway."

So, we went toward the rear and past the wide stairway and down more narrow stairs. After a couple of turns, he led us outside into the fresh air. We then went down the driveway and past buildings and up a hill, until we reached another building. We went inside, where I stood facing another mysterious-looking tunnel not unlike the other one where I'd taken my physical, only this one sloped up instead of down. Later, I learned it was the same tunnel, except I was at the other end.

Before I realized it, he had unlocked a heavy door, and we followed him inside. He turned us over to the energetic attendant, who seemed to be rushing around like mad, and he was gone. So this was a ward in a state hospital. Somehow, it seemed different from what I had expected, although I wasn't sure what I had expected.

Everything seemed hazy, as the attendant took us back through the large room—the day room—and into the small office at the other end. Through the fog in my brain, I was half aware of rocking chairs along both sides of the room. A few old ladies tottered around.

The small office seemed crowded with so many in it. The other attendants appeared to be very busy, but the charge introduced us when she had a chance. She led us back through a hallway to another large room with beds in it. Some beds had patients in them. We took a look and returned to the front.

About that time a tall gray-haired nurse came and got us. She took us on an elevator to a floor upstairs and into a small room where she gave us a lecture. Much of what she told us was a repetition of what Mr. Wright had already told us—that we would have to work two weeks on the 6 to 2 shift in orientation. After that we would be assigned to a shift. We would work in this building during this time and would go to an hour class period in the morning and one in the afternoon. One of the two ward doctors in the building or one of the three nurses in the building, which had 16 wards in it with around 36 patients to a ward, would give us a lecture. The rest of the time, we would work on one of the three women's bed wards.

She told us a lot of things, which seemed to end up as a jumbled up mess. When we entered a building, to the left were always male wards and to the right were female wards, but which was right and which left?

She took us back down stairs, and left some of us on one bed ward and others on another one. I was sent to the one across the hall from the first one. I had another set of attendants to be introduced to. One attendant immediately said to me, "Come with me, and I'll show you how to make a bed." Still dazed, I followed her down the hall past rooms on either side and to the large room filled with a long row of beds on both sides—some with patients in them—and to an empty bed. She showed me how to make a bed—a hospital bed.

While I tried to listen to her instructions, I was conscious of the beds with patients in them. Were they dangerous? The attendant didn't seem to be afraid. Then when we had made that bed, she said, "I'll show you how to give a bed bath and make a bed with a patient in it."

This was something different. I'd be coming in direct contact with the patient. Was she violent? But she seemed to be curled up and unable to help herself. She made no effort to fight us. The attendant washed one side and had me wash the other. We rolled the patient over and put clean sheets on her bed, all the while trying to forget the other occupied beds.

I was half-conscious of a steady unintelligible rumbling around me. The attendants appeared to be in the process of dragging or carrying patients and placing them in the bathtub. There was so much confusion, and things seemed hazy around me. Attendants, all strangers, were running here and rushing there. Patients were jabbering.

One of the attendants said to me, "Come with me." I followed her into the bathroom, where there was a patient being rolled into the old-fashioned bathtub. When she was in there, the attendant gave me a wash cloth, and the first thing I knew, she was gone. I was all alone in the room with the patient trying to grab my hand and bite it, as she let out a blood-curdling scream. Not having yet learned she was blind and paralyzed on one side, I was terrified, expecting the patient to jump from the tub and come after me.

In between times, the charge tried to explain other things. During these two weeks of orientation, we were to pick out two patients that interested us, and we'd have to interview the patient and write up all about them. This scared me; I wasn't sure how to conduct an interview or how to write it up.

I was going to have to write up just how I spent every minute on the ward. We would have to put down just how much of our time we spent feeding patients and how much giving them baths and how much doing housework, like scrubbing and cleaning up, and how much giving medicine and charting and all the other things, and we'd have to turn it into the office. That scared me. I learned that the morning shift always wrote in blue, the afternoon shift wrote in green, and the night shift wrote in red.

The most important thing to remember, however, was that we always signed our names in the order of our seniority.

Anyway, I never had to sign anything. The charge always signed our names in the log book and on the daily report.

Then the gray-haired nurse came and whisked us away to show us some more of the hospital. Just before entering a ward where all the patients were up and moving about, she said, "Don't ever trust any of these patients. They're all treacherous. Don't turn your back on them for a minute."

I entered the ward with the others, not knowing what to expect. These, I thought, will be different from those flat on their backs in bed.

I was surprised, when we were inside and the door was locked behind us, to hear one of the patients who was sitting in one of the old-fashioned high-backed rockers, yell a friendly greeting to the nurse. The nurse, barely turning her head, returned her greeting. Another patient jumped from her rocker and came toward us, also with a pleasant greeting to the nurse. The nurse answered her, as she continued to mosey through the ward. She kidded another patient, who took it in good spirits. I was mixed up. Her actions didn't match her warning, I thought. But I kept right on trying to watch them all with patients on all sides.

We left the ward, and she deposited us on the various bed wards. The food came, and someone told me to feed a patient, who spilled as much on the outside as she did on the inside, her throat muscles being paralyzed.

While some of us were feeding patients, the rest of the attendants had gone to the employees' cafeteria to eat. When they returned, we let them do the cleaning up and we went. Each month $7.50 was deducted from our check for one meal a day, and we paid it whether we ate it or not. But then, 20 or 21 meals for $7.50 couldn't be beat, I thought.

I went with the others to the cafeteria. The small square tables were filled with a motley crowd. Most had on white uniforms, but there were others—the doctors and office workers and others. We picked up our trays and silverware and filled it up and found an empty table. The food was good, I thought, but I heard some complain. The din of conversation around us was terrific. I just ate. I hardly knew what the others were saying. I only heard the noise around me.

When we returned to the ward, a quietness seemed to have settled over the ward. The patients had eaten and seemed quieter. They'd had their baths. Some were in rocking chairs. A few tottered around. Others were still in their beds. By this time, I had decided they didn't look so dangerous. They looked like unfortunate people.

We had to go back to the beds and change some. I was surprised when I heard a voice behind me say, "Oh, how pretty." I turned and saw woman flat on her back and weighing, perhaps, 400 pounds, with a smooth-looking skin and, in a way, pretty.

"That blue uniform," she said, when she saw me looking at her. "I hate white. I'm getting so tired of looking at nothing but white all the time."

It seemed that before I'd had time to turn around, the nurse changed me to the other bed ward and introduced me to about four more attendants. They were in the process of slicking up their ward to get ready to go home, and I noticed one flying around, getting two beds done while the others got one. I was to learn later that one patient had nicknamed her the Speed Demon.

Everybody on this ward was nice to me, the same as they'd been on the other wards. It was as if they had known me for years. But I couldn't remember who was who or what their names were. I'd been introduced to so many people that day. There was so much difference in the atmosphere in this hospital and the other one. The other hospital had a certain amount of quiet reserve and dignity about it; this one was a mad rushing around, and everyone was just one of one big happy family.

All in all, I was feeling pretty good at 2:00 o'clock, when the blast of siren split the air, and the morning shift left, and the afternoon shift took over. But we had come at 8 a.m. instead of 6 a.m. and would have to stay until 4 p.m. So the nurse came and took us upstairs to give us another lecture. When her lecture was finished, and it wasn't quite time for us to leave, she let us go anyway. There was nothing to stay for.

But, as I walked to another building to catch the bus, a funny feeling began to come over me—a shaky inside turmoil. I realized for the first time that day that I was tired. I was going to like working in this hospital, I told myself. Then why this odd sensation? The feeling spread to my whole body. I'll be all right when I get on the bus and sit down, I reasoned.

But when I was settled quietly on the bus, the feeling got stronger. Just being tired couldn't cause this feeling, surely. I had been frightened a few times, but I wasn't now. Everyone had been so nice. I had actually enjoyed myself. I tried to stop the inside shaking. The twisted bodies and grimacing faces seemed to come through the fog in my brain. What had happened during the day to make me feel this way?

Nothing bad, I told myself. I tried to remember. Everything was all garbled up together. To join the union or not to join it was mixed up with the screaming patient in the bathtub. The din in the dining room so I couldn't hear anything that was said at the table where I was sitting was mixed with the patient spitting her food. The hazy picture of a dozen or more attendants—friendly attendants—rushing here and there flooded my thinking.

I tried desperately to get hold of myself. I felt an urge to cry. I fought it down. Then the urge to stand up and scream came over me, and there was no reason for it. I'm just tired, I thought, and will feel better when I get home. No, it was something different from that. It's the work. I can't go back, I thought. I'll never be able to take it. Take what? I didn't know. I couldn't seem to remember what had happened. I'm out of a job. I can't. I can't.

When I got home, I started pacing the floor. Back and forth I went from one room to the other. I can't go back. I can't go back. Still, I couldn't put my finger on the reason. I lay down on the cot, and then, after several minutes of shivering inside, I started to cry. I cried and cried and felt spent when it was over. I felt some better, but I still couldn't see myself going back to the hospital.

But when morning came, and I'd had a night's sleep, I got up and took my bath and rode the bus, feeling a lot better. Still, I was sure I'd never make it for long. I doubted I could take it for more than that. I'll try one more day. I couldn't quit on the second day. I went directly to the ward I was told to go to the night before.

We stood at the door of the ward and at the blast of the whistle, the night shift opened the door and turned her keys over to the charge attendant. We went inside. Things seemed quieter. But I was at a loss to know what to do. While the charge stayed in the office, the rest of us went to the kitchen to wait for the food to arrive. In the meantime, we got out the heavy aluminum trays and put the heavy stainless steel partitioned plates on the trays. Then we filled the heavy aluminum spout cups with the hot coffee the night shift had ready for us. We placed a slice of bread and a spoon full of jelly on each plate.

When the food came in large stainless steel containers, we dished the hot cereal onto the plates. Except for a small dish of apple sauce, that was about what breakfast consisted of.

The next procedure, however, I decided took some special talent. The others started piling the filled trays on a long cart. I tried to help. When I put a tray on the cart, someone would move it. I felt helpless. After loading one layer, they started on another. Then another. Now, I was helpless. The layers got higher and higher, while I watched in fascination. I tensed up, as I waited for the pile to come clattering to the floor.

They stayed right where they were placed, however, as if a magnet were holding them. Even when the cart was pushed clear back to the dormitory, where most of the patients were still in bed, the trays stayed put. The working patients and a few old ladies who were able to walk went to the dining room, which adjoined the kitchen, to eat at the tables.

A tray, with only a large tablespoon for eating, was placed on each bed or the bedside table, which were extremely scarce, and the ones who could feed themselves began. The others we fed, with a few working patients helping us.

When the patients were all fed, the messy trays were loaded back on the cart and returned to the kitchen and scraped. It was then the attendants took a break and toasted themselves some bread and drank a cup of coffee. I sort of got the impression that this wasn't in accordance with the hospital rules. All surplus food was to be scraped up and put in the garbage to be thrown away. But who was going to tell? Many never ate breakfast before they came to work in the mornings.

After that, we were ready to give the baths, and I helped. I watched the charge give medicine. She told us we'd have to do it sometime. Suddenly, I felt afraid. I can't do that. I was also to pick out two patients who interested me and interview them and write up something on them.

In the middle of the morning, a nurse took us upstairs to the nurse's station again and gave us our lecture. We had another one in the afternoon. I went home that day, again feeling tired but not quite so nervous. Still, I wasn't sure just how many days

I'd be able to take it. I worried about having to give the medicine and all the other things. Nevertheless, having stayed on one ward more of the time left me feeling a little less like riding a merry-go-round.

The next morning, I got up early—earlier than necessary—and took my bath. I had to catch the first bus, because it was just nip and tuck for me to make the transfer uptown and get to work on time, and if it was late, I'd be sure to be late.

On Thanksgiving day, I had my holiday, which surprised some, since I'd been there such a short time. Being a 24-hour-day and 365-days-a-year institution, our holidays had to be staggered. The ones with seniority had first choice. But then, our teachers had those days off. Some thought it wasn't fair. I went back to work Friday.

Each day got a little better. I might make it through orientation, after all, I began to think. A few names of attendants and patients began to connect with their faces. Remembering names still bothered me. It's those shock treatments, I thought, and I felt anger toward Dr. Banks fill me. But then, all the attendants seemed nice and friendly. I was actually starting to enjoy myself.

It was also time for me to pick my patients to interview and write about. One little bed-fast lady, who was continually telling us what a terrible sinner she was, interested me. Nothing would pacify her. I had no trouble with her. She seemed to understand the world around her and answered my questions readily. She really was a nice person, I thought.

Another large bony woman, who was in her 90's and nearing the 100-year mark, fascinated me. Besides her age, I was attracted to her because of her extremely bad disposition. She was able to get up and care for herself, and I later learned the attendants were willing to let her do just that. I felt curious. What caused someone to hate the whole world the way she apparently did? At the time, I didn't know that she was the patient the older attendants watched to see how a new attendant would react to her.

I had been given a list of suggested questions, so what I asked her hadn't come entirely from my own imagination. I asked her name and age, and she answered reasonably civilly. Her answers fit the facts, so she seemed to be in contact with reality, I thought. I asked a few more, and I noticed some slight reluctance to answer. I continued. What country was this? Who was our first president? The date? Our present president? I wrote down her answers.

"What place is this?" I asked. It was on the list.

I saw a look come over her face. It was the most hate I had ever seen on one face. "What a dumb question," she sneered, "the State Hospital, of course."

I stepped back, completely cowed. She was right; it was a crazy question. Her anger was justified, I thought. Then I saw another look spread over her face and in her eyes. To me, it looked like compassion. She'd seen my look and was feeling sympathy for me. I felt guilty, and I didn't ask her many questions after that.

I went back to the office and wrote up about her the best way I could. I wasn't much good at anything like this. But the experience did make me think. Was it right to use these patients for guinea pigs to train new employees? There was no need for that information.

We continued to work on the wards and have a lecture each morning and one every afternoon. Sometimes the tall gray-haired nurse gave us the lesson, and other times one of the other two nurses gave it to us. The doctors also took their turn. Dr. X, a jolly man with a foreign accent, was over the male wards in the building. His wife, Mrs. Dr. X, also with a strong foreign accent but not so jolly, also a doctor, was over the female wards,

Our lectures were about almost anything that had to do with our work. We had one on medicine, and the nurse told us they were changing medicine so fast that even she couldn't keep up with it. The doctors were using lots of medicine, especially the tranquilizers, in testing. They got their medicine cheaper that way, I guessed, and state hospitals could be used that way without relatives knowing anything about it. We had lectures on putting on cuffs and belts and straight jackets.

One day, Dr. X was giving us one on ECT, or lobotomy, I wasn't sure which. He started on ECT, and I began to feel nervous; he was touching on a sensitive spot with me. My heart beat faster, but I kept still and listened.

As he talked, he appeared to get more and more excited about his subject. I was also getting more and more nervous.

What was he saying? I wasn't entirely sure. His accent bothered me some. Was I understanding him? I imagined he was opposed to them, but I wasn't sure. I became tense and strained my ears to catch every word.

Then he began to talk about lobotomy operations. Was he saying that they had the same effect as ECT? My anxiety skyrocketed. It seemed as if my heart was about to jump out of my chest. Surely he didn't mean that ECT was as bad as lobotomy. I could hardly breath. That was what it seemed he was saying—that ECT did as much damage as the operation. I hated the shock treatments, but lobotomy was something else again. It really did make robots out of men. I'd read about them.

I began to panic when I heard him say, "I can tell that a person has had ECT 20 years after they've had them." That's what he was saying, all right, that ECT did the same thing to the brain as a lobotomy.

I could stand it no longer and blurted, in a shaky voice, "Do you mean that shock treatments have the same effect on the brain as lobotomy operations?"

He didn't answer me. Instead, he got all excited and began to hurl questions. "Vat you know about shock treatments? Haf you had shock treatments? Vat you know about shock treatments?" I knew I'd made a mistake; I kept still. How could I answer him? Who would have ever thought he'd pounce on that? Could he tell by looking at me that I'd had them? If I keep still, he might shut up.

But he didn't shut up. He kept right on, getting more excited all the time. The other three women's eyes were on me. A kind of anger came over me, and I felt a sudden feeling of so what? What are you going to do about it?

So, in a defiant voice, I said, "Yes, I had nine of them."

Immediately, Dr. X calmed down. He said in a calm voice, "Vell, I vasn't talking about nine; I vas talking about vivty-nine."

He then asked me some questions, and I told him the circumstances and that I hadn't been a patient in this hospital. He seemed not to be condemning me and continued with his lecture in a calm voice. When we left the room and the older woman and I started down the hall in one direction and the sisters in the other, Dr. X came up between us and walked down the hall with us.

With his arms about us, he said, "I hope they put you two women on my wards when they assign you to a ward." He really acted as if he didn't hold it against me that I had doctored with a psychiatrist and had shock treatments, so I didn't worry too much about it.

As the days went by, I got more and more used to the work. I even got so I could do a half-way reasonable job of loading those crazy carts with trays so they wouldn't come clattering to the hard cement floor. Everything seemed to be painted gray—a dark gray. I was beginning to believe I might make it for a while—maybe a year. But when I thought about how long some had been there, I shivered. I'd never last four of five years.

Then, when I had almost finished my two-week orientation, Toby, along with four other boys, got into some trouble with the law. This was even worse than his playing hooky. I was sick. It seemed the world had come to an end. He and the other boys were 16 or younger, so they were all put on probation.

I was still going to Mr. Walters at Family Guidance and talked to him about Toby. He thought Toby might be helped by some counseling, and so did I. Toby was reluctant to go, but he did. However, he went to the Child Guidance part of the center and had a different counselor.

When our two-week orientation was up, we were placed on a regular shift. I had asked for the night shift (from 10 p.m. to 6 a.m.), but, instead, they put me on the 6 to 2 shift. I had wanted the night shift because I felt it would make it easier to care for Cynthia and Edward.

What baffled me was that one of the two young women had asked for the morning shift, and they put her on the afternoon shift. Barb, her sister, had asked for the afternoon shift, and they gave her the morning shift. The other lady, who had worked ten years in Colorado at a state hospital on the night shift, asked for that shift, and they gave it to her. I remembered how I had been hired for a specific shift at the other hospital, and they had waited until they had an opening on that shift. It so happened that Barb and I were placed on the same bed ward as regulars in the morning.

Chapter 9

Problems at Work

I had a problem. Since this hospital seemed to prefer to give us exactly what we didn't want, I had to hunt up a permanent baby sitter. The temporary one wasn't too convenient. Mr. Walters at Family Guidance solved it for me. He suggested we go to a house that was connected with them in some way and was also partially funded by the United Fund. They had a limit of 28 children and we just barely got in for that. It was near where Phil worked, and he could take them as he went to work, and I could get them when I got off, by riding the bus. It was cheap—$1.50 per child per day. Since I had my two off days in the middle of the week, I only had to pay for three days. I had built-in baby sitters for Saturday and Sunday. Nine dollars a week would make it $36 for the month. With the $7.50 for meals, I wouldn't be getting much more at this hospital in the end than the other one—about nine dollars. But I would have that extra day off.

From then on my duties were about the same as they'd been in orientation, except I wouldn't have to go to those lectures. Several attendants warned me that I would be on probation for six months, and, during that time, I'd better be extra careful. I could be fired for practically nothing, and I would have no way to fight it. At the end of the six months, I would be put on as a regular and would have the right to go to the state capitol and fight it there through the Merit System.

But as the days went by, and I was liking my work, I wasn't too worried. It was much better than the work at the other hospital. I liked the attendants and was catching on to the work. I felt sure I was doing my share. The charge, Mrs. Anderson, seemed a little rattled at times, and she couldn't spell worth anything, but she was nice. I liked Josephine very well, and Pearl was a live-wire and friendly, but it was next to impossible to keep up with her when she worked. Speed Demon, the patients called her. Both these women had worked for about a year, and Mrs. Anderson had been there about five years. I liked Barb, who had started the same time I had.

I got over the fear of the bed patients, but we did have working patients coming from the other ward. I got to know these patients, also, and I didn't feel uneasy working with them. Most of our help came from the diabetic or epileptic wards, and a few came from the ward across the hall which might have been called the neurotic ward, if there was such a thing. It was sort of a mixture of patients who didn't seem to fit on some of the other wards. Nevertheless, some were definitely psychotic.

Orpha Spencer from the ward across the hall, however, for some reason—punishment or something—was on our ward for the time being. She was pacing the floor from the exit light in the rear of the dormitory to the outside wire gate leading to the outside hall, which was always kept locked. As she passed the office doorway, she would stop and curse and threaten. She had a headache, she claimed, and wanted a couple of aspirins. I didn't know why Mrs. Anderson was refusing to give her one, but she was.

She raved and carried on so much that Mrs. Anderson finally called the nurse and got permission to give the aspirin. She gave me the two tablets and told me to take them to Orpha.

Almost paralyzed with fear, I took the two white tablets, and made my way to the outside wire gate, where Orpha stood with her fingers grasping the wire gate, while she raved and cursed. This patient is really insane, I thought. All my life, I had been scared of crazy people, although I had never actually seen one. I had only heard stories about how some raving maniac had committed some heinous crime. I had sort of stopped thinking about these little ladies curled up helplessly in bed as insane.

But Orpha was different. She was on her feet, and the way she sounded, she could have done anything. But I had my orders, and I had been told I must follow orders and never complain. So I walked to the hall, leaving the others safely in the office, and gave Orpha her medicine. She took it calmly without a word. I hurried back to the office.

Then there was Audrey, another patient from the ward across the hall, who came to work with the laundry. She was so quiet I hardly knew she existed. But one day she became talkative and was continually wanting someone to look at her neck to see if they could see the snake bites on it. That's what they called being disturbed—or "blowed."

I was in the bathroom when I felt a tap on my shoulder and turned to see Audrey standing there with her finger on her lip. She said "Sh! Sh! Don't look now, but there's snakes in the bathtub."

Terror seized me, but I said quietly, "Let's get out of here then; I don't like snakes."

I opened the door, which she had pulled shut after her as she entered, and she followed outside willingly. After that, I watched carefully not to let her get me cornered in a room with the door shut behind her.

Gertrude was another patient who came over to our ward from across the hall to work, or what was supposed to be work, along with several others. They had the job of polishing the gray cement floors after they'd been waxed. To do this, they used heavy wooden blocks wrapped with some old worn-out woolen blankets with broom handles fastened on them. Around and around, they pushed these blocks. Sometimes, I thought they had these patients do this, not because it needed doing, but for the purpose of giving the patient something to do that matched their mentality. The patients all went in one direction, except Gertrude. She would, invariably, turn and go the other way and bump into the others. She would have to be turned around.

One little white-haired lady seemed to think she was running the place, and she would write the attendants checks on toilet paper. No one asked her to do anything, but she would get her a small block and wrap it and push along with the others. She wasn't very big, but she could get really sassy, and I didn't relish tangling with her.

We had another white-haired woman who was on the ward for a broken hip. She was bossy, too, and sat in her bed, giving orders right and left. Otherwise, I thought she seemed fairly normal and in contact with things around her. I wondered why she was there.

I wondered no more when one morning she started telling me about a big fire in New York. At first, I thought she had read something in the paper that I hadn't. Then she went on to tell about a similar fire in Chicago. I listened in fascination while she told about hurricanes, tornadoes and more fires in all the large cities in the world. London, Paris, San Francisco, Tokyo, St. Louis were all being destroyed by some big catastrophe. Everything was going. The whole world was being destroyed by earthquakes, storms or fires. Then she added with no show of emotion or guilt, "I did it all. I was the cause of it."

I also learned that mental patients could be downright lovable. There was little Julie, who was paralyzed from her waist down and didn't know one attendant from another. She'd lie in her bed and watch us with big saucer eyes and scold us and tell us how to do our work. She'd shake her finger at us in anger if we didn't suit her. She kept two dolls with her that she called Peter and Ralph. She'd pull their clothes off, and when the attendants told her they might get pneumonia, her eyes would get wide open and she'd drawl, "D'you reckon?" All the attendants loved her, in spite of their having to care for her like a baby.

There were others who were repulsive, like the ones who filled their mouths with BM or threw it at the wall or attendants or other patients. Usually, most of the attendants had a lot of patience with these and even felt some affection for them. I heard of one attendant who was unable to keep her own meals down for about a week after she started work, but later she said she could sit right down in the middle of it and eat a meal.

There were those who stirred up compassion in the hearts of those who cared for them, like the ones twisted up with arthritis and covered with bed sores. Huntington's Chorea, I thought, was a pathetic disease.

Then there were those—some were more senile than anything else—whose minds were all mixed up. Their mixed up answers and garbled speech made it fun for the attendants to ask them questions and talk to them for the purpose of hearing what they would say. At first I saw nothing wrong with this, since the patient, as well as the attendant, seemed to be enjoying it. They seemed unaware of what was going on.

Then, one day the attendants had been talking to Elsie Annette, a seizure patient as well as very retarded and with some mixed up ideas about sex, and asking her a lot of questions. Suddenly she stopped and said, "I'm not going to say any more. You're just making fun of me." I realized they knew more than it might seem they knew. Laughing with the patients was different from laughing at them, although there were times when the patients came up with such good ones it was impossible not to see the humor in it. It was like our kids saying cute things.

There was one thing I learned to believe—that it would be terribly hard for anyone to work in a state hospital who didn't have a sense of humor. But I did think that the patient's feelings should be considered. I was, somehow, identifying with the patient.

There was something about the work that was worrying me. We were told we would have to take our turn giving the medicine to the 36 patients, some who didn't even know their names. We would have to set it up and give it and chart it. I was scared. I still had trouble remembering names. I still blamed it onto the ECT. There were so many names, and they wouldn't stick in my mind.

Then there were all those different shapes and colors of pills and capsules. Everything looked so complicated. Some patients got two and three kinds. But Barb didn't look worried and nervous, and she didn't seem to have the trouble remembering names I did. But then she was younger than I was—about 18 years younger.

I tried my best to remember the names and which name to put with which patient. I was practically holding my breath waiting for the time when I would have to give the medicine.

Finally, the day came when Mrs. Anderson told Barb it was her turn to give it for a week. I was secretly relieved. I would have another week to study the names. Yet, the time was getting closer.

I was mistaken. When Barb finished her week, Mrs. Anderson had one of the other women take her turn again. Now I was hurt. I had been worried, but this was a slap in the face. It was as if the charge was saying to me, "You can't. I don't believe you have it in you. You can do ordinary work but not important things."

I lived my early life all over again, when Amelia could do everything, but all I could do was the measly jobs. I'm a failure. I didn't even have a chance to try. Had her oversight been deliberate, or had it been an accident? I pacified myself that it had been the latter. At least, I thought, it will give me more time to learn the patients' names better.

But when they made the rounds again, and I was skipped over, I knew it was no accident. She was deliberately telling me I couldn't. To make matters worse, she called me into the locker room with about 45 steel lockers holding the patient's clothing, and, while Barb was giving the medicine, she had me take the clothing out of each one, scrub it out and return the belongings to the locker. There was a lump in my throat, while I reasoned that as soon as Barb finished giving the medicine, she would come and help me.

But she never came. She finished giving her medicine, and then I heard them taking a break after they had finished with their work. While I scrubbed, I heard them laughing and talking. I could understand the older ones getting a break and not having to do the dirty work, but Barb had no more seniority than I had. Why didn't she have her, at least, help me? It didn't make sense. I could understand her name going above mine and her seemingly being above me in everything, like getting her turn first on giving medicine, since her name was ahead of mine alphabetically. But this was different. I wasn't even getting a turn at all.

I was having trouble keeping the tears from coming to my eyes. Mrs. Anderson came into the room herself a time or two and helped a little to make sure I'd get finished by the time for us to go home. But even that didn't help. It was the principal of the thing. She was deliberately playing favorite. Barb should have helped. I was just the scrub woman. Barb was younger than I was, but not that young. She was about 28 and should have been in the prime of life. I was 46. The other three women were in their 50's.

I was finding it hard to take. But what could I do? I had been told I must obey orders and never complain, no matter what came up. What would Dr. Banks say? That I was eating worms? Mr. Walters at Family Guidance was doing his best to keep up my self-confidence, but sometimes it got pretty low. I was a failure. All anyone had to do was to look at me, and they knew I was.

Still, when I went home and had forgotten about this deal—at least put it out of my mind—I went on with my work. I wasn't too miserable.

Then it happened again that Mrs. Anderson told me to clean out the lockers. Again, she had me do it alone without having Barb help me. This was almost too much for me. Tears did come to my eyes, but I kept my face hidden and didn't let anyone see. It was no use. I must face it. I was inferior to everyone. If I wanted a job, I would have to be satisfied with the menial jobs. Something was wrong with me, and I didn't know what. My high IQ that Dr. Banks said I had couldn't help me out on this. It took more than brains to be a success. I went home that day with a determination to take what was handed to me and say nothing.

My heart almost stood still one day when Mrs. Anderson told me I would have to give the medicine. She stayed with me while I set it up the first time and then went with me while I passed it out. I felt awkward and unsure of myself. I felt still more anxiety when she turned me loose and let me do it on my own. I had never been much of a pill taker. Mama had been unusually afraid of medicine and wouldn't let Amelia and me even take an aspirin for menstrual pains. I respected pills. One of the exceptions was a laxative, and, although I had grown up on caster oil, Epsom salts and syrup of figs, I never took a laxative anymore. Those 56 little cone cups filled with all colors, sizes, shapes of pills and capsules looked to me almost as dangerous as a box full of copperheads, rattlesnakes or cobras.

Besides my over-conscientiousness, I was having trouble seeing the labels on the bottles. Doing ordinary work gave me no trouble, but, like when I took the tests and had trouble hurrying, I was again hampered with my aging far-sighted eyes. I was slow and knew it. I realized I wasn't getting the medicine passed out as fast as the others. After a couple of days of this, Anderson told me about it. I must speed up, and I tried.

I didn't feel too concerned when, a few days later, I was called to the main office and Mrs. Best, the head supervisor, told me I was too slow, but she was nice about it. I told her about my eyes bothering me, but that just as soon as I got my check, which was only a day or so away, I would have my eyes tested and get some glasses. Then she told me I was wearing my hair too long. I promised her I would get it cut and get a permanent, even though I knew my hair never took a good permanent. I thought that took care of it.

At that time, I made no connection between this criticism and the ward doctor's apparent dislike for me and Mrs. Anderson's giving me the dirty work and Barb the more responsible work.

The ward doctor (Mrs. Dr. X) had shown little friendliness toward any of the attendants, I'd thought, but her coldness to me was much worse than it was toward the rest. At least, she did speak to them. She ignored me and looked over my head and seemed not even to see me. Maybe she had sensed my irritation toward the rule that we were supposed to stand up in the presence of our superiors like the doctors and nurses and supervisors and even the charges. Maybe that was the reason she didn't like me, I reasoned.

I had even told some how I felt about that rule. It might have gotten back to her. I knew she was terribly strong in believing that we inferiors should give the superiors special respect.

I was perfectly willing to respect authority and superior education and training and knowledge for itself. But standing up in deference to their position was something else. It was like bowing down to kings and queens. Maybe other countries demanded that, but this was United States, where all of us were considered to be equals. I simply couldn't see standing up only for special people. As persons, attendants were no different from supervisors or nurses.

Nevertheless, although Mrs. Dr. X seemed not to like me, her husband, Dr. X, was his own friendly good-natured self. He seemed to hold no grudge against me and always had a smiling greeting for me as well as the others. So, I didn't worry too much about his wife's antagonism toward me.

Anyway, I was an independent thinker, although I was not very brave when it come to acting. I wasn't too courageous in standing up to my beliefs. I was scared of people, and usually tried to obey orders, even though I might not entirely believe in the orders.

Still, I had my thoughts, and they didn't always seem to jibe with the way others thought. I was an independent thinker. Maybe that's what Dr. Banks had meant when he said, when I had asked him about using hypnotism in therapy for mental illness, "I don't believe in hypnotism for that. It might be all right in dentistry and such but not for mental illness." Then, he had added, "Anyway, you couldn't be hypnotized. You're too cynical. You're like me."

So that was the way I thought; I lived in The United States and wasn't bowing down to anyone. The doctor wasn't even a citizen of our country at the time. Yet, I wasn't prejudiced against naturalized citizens, and the doctors had started proceedings to become citizens. My dad, being a Swedish immigrant, was a naturalized citizen.

Anyway, I did recognize authority, and when I got my check, I went to the eye doctor and got a pair of glasses and at the same time that day, I had them put on a chain around my neck. I was also sporting a new permanent. Josephine, Mrs. Anderson, Barb and I were in the dormitory giving the beds and the patients their last slicking up before going home and turning it all over to the afternoon shift.

I was nearest the door with the others scattered over the ward when Mrs. Steinman, the building supervisor, pranced in and stopped near me and started raking me ever the coals about my hair. Completely taken aback since I had gotten my permanent and my hair cut, when she stopped long enough to take a breath, I gasped stupidly, "I got a permanent." She ignored that and started in on me about my eyes and how bad it was to take a chance on giving the wrong medicine.

I was still stunned and said, "But I got my glasses."

She then hit me harder than ever. The patients weren't getting the care they should. They were dehydrated something awful, she raved at me. I could find no answer for that one. She was making it sound as if we did nothing for the patients. We fed them. We gave then baths. They got their medicine and their beds changed when they wet them. I didn't know about the dehydration. I hadn't thought of that. I had only followed orders, and I had given them water. But maybe it hadn't been enough.

I just stood there and listened, stupefied. I couldn't even wonder why I was responsible for all that, if it were true. I had less seniority than all the others, except Barb, and why wasn't she as responsible as I was?

I stood immobilized, trying to make some sense out of it. I was getting pounded over the head and didn't know why. I had only been taking orders. I had been told that was what I must do. She stopped raving as suddenly as she had started and turned and left the room. I watched her retreating figure down the hall in a daze. A sudden thought hit me. Mrs. Dr. X was behind it all. Although Dr. X was nice and jolly, he no doubt had told his wife about my doctoring with a psychiatrist and having had ECT. I knew, now, why she didn't like me.

Almost immediately, the other three women were by my side, asking me excitedly what it was all about. I couldn't tell them. I couldn't even talk. I was as baffled as they were and more hurt and scared. This, I thought, was the end of my job.

I had stood, dry-eyed, while Mrs. Steinman had been raving furiously, but when the other attendants rushed up to me in apparent sympathy, I was unable to keep the tears from my eyes. I was all choked up. The tears increased, as we walked to the office with the other women talking and wondering what had brought on the supervisor's tirade. It was so ridiculous. It was as unclear to them as it was to me.

In fact, it was more so. I had sort of figured it out. I told them what I thought, but they didn't seem so sure. But I was sure. There could have been no other reason. Jumping onto me about the care of the patients was so unreasonable that there had to be some other reason. If I had defied their orders and told Mrs. Best I wouldn't get glasses or try to do better on the other, there might have been a reason. But I had tried to do everything they told me to do.

Josephine and Barb went into the office and sat down. Mrs. Anderson sat at the desk. I stood in the doorway. I was in no mood to sit down. I was crying now. Josephine and the charge talked and tried to make sense from it, while Barb just sat and watched me in sympathy, apparently trying to grasp the meaning of it all.

Mrs. Anderson said, "Call over to the main office and ask to talk to Mrs. Best. Ask her what it is all about."

"But I know what it's all about. Mrs. Dr. X is trying to get me fired because I had ECT."

Barb said nothing, and Josephine didn't seem so sure that going to the head supervisor would be the best, but the charge insisted.

"But I'm not fit to go over there and face her with my eyes so red," I said. "It will just make things worse, and, in my condition, I won't be able to talk."

She still insisted and finally said, "If I call over there and ask her to let you go over and talk to her, will you go?" After some time and still leery of the wisdom of going, I agreed. She called, and Mrs. Best said for me to come on over. I went.

When I walked into the main office and tried to tell the head supervisor what had happened, she lit in on me so hard that the building supervisor's tirade looked mild in comparison. I couldn't take instruction. But how hadn't I taken instructions, I wondered? I had done everything I had been told to do.

It didn't take me long to know she had one plan in her mind—get rid of me. It was for one reason. It was no use. The job was gone anyway. I became determined to face her with the truth.

"Was all this brought about because I had doctored with a psychiatrist and had shock treatments?" I asked, by this time not really caring.

She seemed a little taken aback and said, in a sort of surprise, "I didn't know you had."

Somehow I believed her innocence was genuine. She really hadn't heard. She calmed down now, and I told her a little of the circumstances. I hadn't been a patient in this hospital, I assured her.

About that time, I became aware of someone standing in the doorway. I looked up and saw the nice supervisor who had taken me across the grounds to take my physical. A few seconds later, I saw Phil standing there. I had forgotten this was Sunday, and since the busses didn't run so often, he always came after me.

I introduced Mrs. Best to him, and she invited him inside. She was a lot nicer now. Yet, after we had explained the situation to him, she said to Phil, "Don't you think this work is too hard for her? Shouldn't she get something else that won't make her so nervous? This work is making her worse."

Phil said, "I don't think so. I think it has helped her." There was nothing for her to say to that. Then Phil said, "There is one thing I do know. No boss where I work would dare to bawl anyone out in front of the other employees. If she did deserve correction, she should have been taken someplace alone and told about it. We have a union down there."

We had a union, too, and I had joined it, in spite of some refusing because they were afraid to join. The personnel manager said they wouldn't be fired, but they didn't believe it. I was sure my joining the union had nothing to do with this, because the union had no power and could do nothing about it. There were too many who were afraid.

Anyway, Mrs. Best said, "You come back to work as usual tomorrow. I'll call over to the ward about nine o'clock and have you go over to Mr. Wright's office."

I wasn't sure what this meant, but it didn't sound good to me. I began to wonder if I could get my other job back at the other hospital. I was afraid I couldn't. But then there was the other hospital; they might hire me.

I didn't feel much better when I came to work the next morning and all the attendants had heard about it. They said,

"You've had it. When you're sent to Mr. Wright, it means you're fired."

I was feeling pretty low at first, but as the time passed, I became used to the idea. I would just have to hunt up something else. I went about my work quietly, saying little, but I was terribly conscious of the time.

At nine, I was expecting the call, but no call came. At 9:50, I was still waiting. No call came. I wondered what had happened. At 10:00, I was waiting, and also at 10:50. I was getting more and more resigned to getting fired. For what? For having seen a psychiatrist? I knew I had done nothing to deserve it. I had been doing my share of the work and maybe more. After the meals, when the other attendants went into the office for a break and Elsie Annette was back in the dormitory sweeping up the crumbs, I would go back with her and, while she swept one side of the aisle, I would sweep the other side. While some of the others were still goofing off, I would be the first one to start the baths. It made no difference. I had been warned that during the first six months I could get fired for anything or nothing at all.

I waited and waited, and no call had come. It was almost time for the food to come for lunch, and I was bathing a patient when I looked toward the rear of the room and saw Mrs. Best and another supervisor come through the exit door. Upon reaching me, they stopped. Mrs. Best asked me how I was and a few more nice questions. She said nothing about my going to see Mr. Wright. She walked on and talked to the charge.

Later, Mrs. Anderson told me what Mrs. Best said to her. She asked Mrs. Anderson how I was feeling, who told her I seemed to be feeling some better. Then Mrs. Best had said, "I think she's all right. Help her all you can."

I was hurt by her last statement. Why should I need more help than the others. Sure, Mrs. Anderson had more experience than I had, but was she so much smarter than I was? In fact, I had sort of wondered about her intelligence, although I knew anyone taking the Merit Test couldn't be completely dumb.

One day, she asked me to count the sheets on the shelves in the linen room. It only took me a minute or two to count 19 full piles and one pile with 11 sheets in it. I knew a full pile had 18 sheets in it and quickly multiplied 20 times 18 and subtracted 7 from it. She had a blank look on her face when I returned so quickly, and she asked me how many piles there were and then asked me how I got the answer. I told her and she still looked confused. Then she got a pen and paper and multiplied 19 times 18 and added 11 to it. She said nothing, and I said nothing, but I thought it didn't take a genius to figure that out.

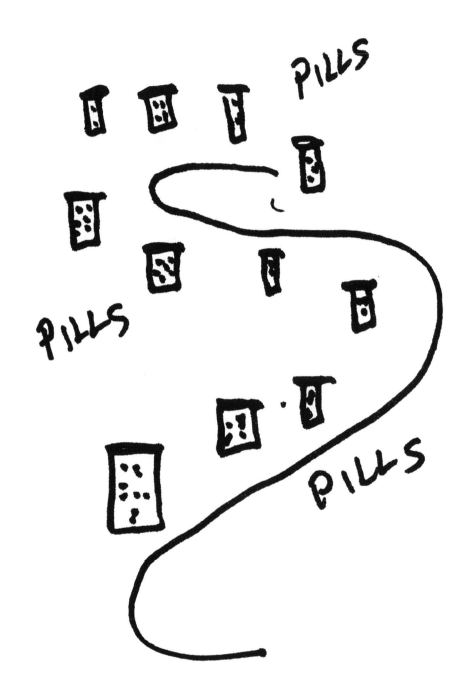

Chapter 10

Juggling Work and Home

Soon after the hospital's attempt to fire me, I was moved to another ward—another bed ward—one that had a different doctor over it. It could be, I supposed, that was one way of keeping Mrs. Doctor X quiet. She had no jurisdiction over this other ward. Or else, I thought, she might have put me under a different charge, so as to get an evaluation of my ability from a charge who was more in with the head supervisors.

I started riding to work with Mrs. Wheeler, my new charge. I learned she was firm and strict, but I did think she was more fair than Mrs. Anderson had been.

At first I did the hard and dirty work on this ward without complaining, feeling lucky I even had a job. Then, one day, on tub bath day, Mrs. Wheeler had an errand to run, and Gladys, who was good at getting out of some of the harder work, piped up, "I will."

"Oh, no, you won't," Mrs. Wheeler answered quickly, "Eastman is going this time."

When I had completed that errand and had returned to the ward, Mrs. Wheeler had another one for me. I did that one while the others gave baths, but when I had finished with it, she greeted me with another one. I didn't help with the bathing at all that day. Instead, I had been running all over the hospital grounds—to take a patient to staff or to the beauty parlor or to the dentist. I wondered, had she been watching and was aware I was getting the dirty jobs?

Not long after I was moved, Mrs. Best came on the ward and asked to talk to me. Discreetly she took me to a side room, where none of the other employees or any of the patients could hear. So, I thought, what Phil had said to her had sunk in. She told me that Mr. Wright was ordering me to go to Howard, the head psychologist, and take some tests

I was to go the next day, my day off. The huge wet flakes of snow floated to the ground, melting as fast as it came down, on my way to the hospital. I went to the same building where I had gone to see Dr. Banks in the past, and this was his day to be there in the afternoon. It so happened Dr. Howard had a conference to attend, so he turned me over to a Mr. Orlando and let him give it.

When Mr. Orlando arrived, he began to look on shelves and in drawers, seemingly having forgotten where his material was.

Finally, be came up with some papers and sat down at the desk and began to give me the test. After I finished the first one, he said, sounding a little surprised, "You came out good on that one." I said nothing.

He continued with the testing, going from one type of tests to another, without making any comment, until we came to the one with the colored blocks, and I said, "Oh, I've done that one before." He suddenly sat up straight in his chair and said, "What in the world brought on all this?"

I then told him about my going to Dr. Banks and having had ECT and about Dr. X learning about it and about his wife trying to get me fired. I was sure she was behind the raking over the coals I'd gotten by the supervisors, I told him. I didn't know her motive, I told him, but maybe she was jealous of any other doctor besides herself being able to rehabilitate any patient. He appeared disgusted.

"You go and talk to Mr. Wright," he said and then changed it and said, "No, I'll go and talk to him; you go and talk to your doctor."

When I left after finishing the tests, Mr. Orlando said, "They might want you to take some more tests, but I think this is the last you'll hear about this."

Dr. Banks wouldn't be there until afternoon, so I went over to my regular ward and helped with the work, feeding patients and cleaning up, while waiting for him. I saw no reason for going home and making another trip. Anyway, by this time, it was snowing much harder, and the wind had gotten much stronger, and the temperature had dropped considerably.

In the afternoon, I took the tunnel to the intensive treatment building. Now it was really blowing and snowing, having turned into a regular blizzard. I waited for some time, then learned that Dr. Banks wasn't coming. It was storming much worse where he was than where I was.

When I came the next week and told him what had happened he accused me of being a nut or something for telling it, and I told him I had to say something when Dr. X had been so persistent.

"If I had thought you were too unstable to do this work, I would never have encouraged you to take it," he told me, and when it was time for me to leave, he said, "If anyone tries to fire you for no reason at all, let me know, and I'll straighten somebody's thinking out."

I left, feeling much better and more secure, although I wasn't sure how much power he had to help me out, even though he did tell me, with a mischievous gleam in his eyes, that he was going to chew the rag with our superintendent for a while. What was he going to say to him, I wondered? Would he have some influence on whether I got fired or not, but, then, I'd thought Mr. Orlando was going to stop that.

Even though I went back to work feeling that I had someone to back me, I took no chances and worked harder than ever. I seemed to have gotten in good with Mrs. Wheeler, and even

Mrs. Best seemed to take a different attitude toward me. I almost believed, at times, I was Mrs. Steinman's favorite.

I seemed to be changing my days off continually to suit someone else, and one day after I had agreed to change, Mrs. Steinman said, "I'm glad there's somebody who's easy to please."

It so happened that I now had both tub bath days off, seemingly the hardest days. We were discussing it one day, and when Gladys learned I had those days off, she began to complain and said, "It isn't fair."

I tried to explain how it had happened, but she still said, "It's still not right." They talked on, still not liking it because I'd ended up with both tub bath days off. But I didn't care. If it bothered them so much, I was willing to change. All I asked was that I not have Saturday and Sunday off. I told Mrs. Steinman that some of the attendants seemed to think I was getting it too easy by having the two hard days off. I was willing to change, I told her, so as to please them.

A few days later, the nice supervisor came and asked me if I wanted to change. I told her that some thought it wasn't fair and that I was having it too easy.

"Are you satisfied with your days," she asked.

"As far as I'm concerned I am, but I don't want to make the others think I'm being pampered. I really don't care, except for Saturday and Sunday."

"If you're satisfied, you're going to keep them," she assured me.

In the meantime, while I was getting all these problems settled at work, I had been going to see Mr. Walters at Family Guidance once or twice a month to help me solve some of my family problems that seemed too much for me. It had bothered me some when I had changed from the first counselor, a quick, plainspoken, small man, to him, who was tall and reserved.

I got to know Mr. Walters, however, and really liked him better than I had the first counselor. Yet, I never seemed to form the close rapport, or dependence, on either one that I had on Dr. Banks. They were like friends, helping to solve some of my problems.

Then Mr. Walters went into the service, but he seemed to think I should continue with Family Guidance a while longer and turned me over to another worker. I had the same trouble getting adjusted to him, but in time I did, and he helped me by talking about my dreams, and I learned from them a little of what was bothering me and how to interpret some of their hidden subtle meanings. Then, he also left for a better job in another state, and I quit going to Family Guidance.

I seemed to be getting along fairly well on my new ward, although there was one thing that I didn't like too well. Mrs. Anderson had insisted that whoever gave the medicine charted it. But on this ward, anyone could chart it and initial it for the one who had given it, although we each took our turns a week at a time giving the medicine. I noticed that Gladys had a way of finding time to dash into the office and chart the medicine while the rest of us were busy. She got out of some hard dirty work that way, it seemed.

One day, I happened to be charting my own medicine and suddenly realized I hadn't given the medicine the way it was charted the day before. We always just looked at the way it was the day before and charted it that way. I was scared. I must have given the wrong medicine. I'd better make sure, I thought, and looked on the medicine card, but, according to it, I had given the right medicine. So I went to the Doctor's Order Sheet. It also read the same way I had given it. It evidently had been being given correctly all the time, but it had been charted wrong day after day. So I ignored the way it had been charted the day before and charted it the way I had given it.

After that, I charted the medicine the way I had given it each day, ignoring the others' charting, thinking they'd catch on in tine. But they didn't; they ignored mine and continued to do it wrong. I said nothing. Neither did they until one day Mrs. Wheeler said, while sitting at the desk and looking over some charts, "What's wrong, Eastman? You've been charting all wrong."

"Well, Eastman," Gladys said, in an important tone of voice. "It looks as if you've been here long enough to know better than that." So they've finally found it, I thought. But why say I was wrong?

A sudden anger flashed through me because of the way Gladys had said it. She could always sound so important. But this time she was wrong, I was sure, so I stood up and looked over Mrs. Wheeler's shoulder and saw for sure it was that patient's chart. I pulled the medicine card and said, "That's the way it is on the medicine card. That's the way I gave it, and that's the way I charted it."

I then showed her the Doctor's Order Sheet and said, "That's the way the doctor ordered it, and that's the way I gave it, and that's the way I charted it."

Mrs. Wheeler said not a word, and even Gladys was silent. Oh, how I would have loved to have said something sarcastic to Gladys, but I kept still.

Another day, Gladys had charted my medicine. I had given one patient an extra pill for her stomach—one that wasn't her usual medication. Later, while Gladys and I were in the dormitory working, Mrs. Steinman came to us and, sounding puzzled, said "I can't figure out what makes Helen's emesis so dark."

"Maybe, it's from the little green pill I gave her," I suggested.

"You never gave her any green pill," Gladys retorted quickly.

"I most certainly did," I said.

"It's not charted," the building supervisor said, appearing a little puzzled.

"You didn't give any pill," Gladys insisted.

"I gave it all right. The doctor ordered it, and I gave it, but I didn't chart it. Someone else did the charting." I was feeling slightly angry. I added, "It's in a bottle just to the right of the other medicine in the medicine cabinet."

Mrs. Steinman turned and went to the office. Soon she was back and said, "You're right. It is ordered and is in a bottle just where you said it was."

Gladys could be nice if she wanted to be, but she was pretty bossy. She was, however, one attendant I could stand up to. When she got out of line, I would snap back at her, and she would straighten out.

The patients, also, seemed to see her as too bossy, because one day, the tall gray-haired nurse came to me and said, referring to a working patient, "Della refuses to come down here and work if she has to work with Gladys. Would you talk to Della and explain to her that it's just Gladys' way? Tell her not to pay any attention to Gladys."

Now I was the one confused. Why did the nurse come to me and ask me to do it? Why didn't she do it herself or have the charge do it? Or better yet, why didn't she go to Gladys and tell her? Why did she expect the patient to understand the attendant? Why not the attendant understand the patient? I wondered which one was the patient.

I didn't know what to say to the nurse, and I wasn't sure how I would go about telling the patient. But the situation was solved when they found a job for the patient where she wouldn't have to work with Gladys.

I wasn't having trouble with the patients' wanting to work with me. Each attendant was supposed to have a patient working with her to carry the water and hold the patient on the other side of the bed so she wouldn't fall. As soon as the working patients entered the ward, they would all make a dive for me, and I would be in the center unable to move. I could only have one.

I wasn't sure whether this was good or bad. Was I identifying with the patient too much? Maybe they acted that way because I wouldn't ask a patient to do anything I wouldn't do myself, and I wasn't bossy.

One day, Chuck came home, saying he wanted a paper route; his high school buddy was quitting his and wanted Chuck to take it over. This scared me. Phil and I would have to sign something, and I wasn't sure what that would mean. We'd had one experience with the J. R. Watkins Company, and I didn't want another experience like that one. At the same time, Henry had decided he wanted a paper route and had gone up to the publishers and put in his application.

So when the cute lady came to interview us, she couldn't decide which boy had first rights, so she gave each one a route. Phil and I had done a lot of thinking it over before signing for them.

That was a job getting both boys up to send them off in time to get the papers thrown before school. Both boys did all right, but Chuck didn't seem to like it so well and didn't keep on too long. I guessed he didn't like the cranky customers, or maybe it was just having to crawl out of bed so early. But, then, he had enough with his school and ROTC. His buddy had also gotten him into the Honor Guard, and he had to go to the games and things. But Henry kept right on with his and did a good job. Occasionally, I had to carry a paper that he had missed and he was gone to school.

Although I was feeling a lot better and more sure of my job, I still lacked a lot of self-confidence. There were still times when I felt the sting of being inferior to the others. One Sunday I came to work, and there were only two of us there and no more help to send. Shirley, the other girl, had a couple of months less seniority than I had. By rights and according to the rules, I should have taken the responsibility as charge. I was scared, believing that I would have to do it. Working under someone and being boss were two different things. I was saved, however, when Shirley smartly announced, "They told me I was to be charge."

Now I felt hurt. I was saved the responsibility, but at the same time, my ego took a nose-dive. I was so inferior the supervisors didn't even trust me to do what was really mine to do. But then I passed it off as unimportant. We both knew what to do, and Sunday was really the easiest day, except for relatives coming. Relatives seldom came, and if they did, it was usually on the afternoon shift, after 2:00 p.m.

We fed the patients and cleaned up the mess, while Shirley kept leaving, saying she had something to do in relation to her job as charge. I was unable to understand what she had to do. No doctors came on Sunday, and the nurses were scarce.

With that over, I loaded the cart with sheets, open hospital gowns, rags, bed mats, bath towels, pails of water, soap and all the other necessary items. Shirley gave the medicine, but when she was finished, I expected her to help me with the baths. She did say something about giving the baths in the side rooms, but somehow, I was a little skeptical of her even giving those. I was suspicious she was letting the working patients do it for her. They were only supposed to help.

Even if she had given them herself, it shouldn't take her so long. There were eight patients in the side rooms, and I had 28 in the dormitory to bathe. I gave one bath after another, and she didn't come back and help me. I knew she was having herself the time of her life, with all that freedom to go and do as she pleased. She was charge, and she was living it up. And she had less seniority than I had.

The time was going by, and it was almost time for lunch to arrive. I hurried to get done. When I had two patients left, she came and gave the one a few swipes with a wet rag. Frankly I was disgusted, and yet, I took it without a complaint. I guessed it was what Dr. Banks meant when he said I was eating worms. But I couldn't fight.

Then one day I came to work, and none of the others had come to work. Again fear shot through me. The work didn't bother me when I had someone else to take the responsibility. Here I was, all alone. I was sure I couldn't do it by myself, but I was even afraid to have to report this to the office. But there was nothing else for me to do, and they sent me a nice quiet attendant who had worked this ward, but she had less seniority than I had.

There was nothing important-acting about this one, so we fed the patients and cleaned up and then started in on the bed baths. I took one side and she took the other side, with a working patient with each one of us. She never said they told her to be charge, so I guessed I was. But I knew nothing about this charge business, so I went to work doing what I usually did and we worked side by side, neither of us as charge.

If a supervisor came on the ward, I kept on working the way I always had and didn't march with them as though they didn't know their way around. They knew where to find us, I reasoned, and certainly wouldn't get lost. The woman working with me was quiet and friendly and efficient and unobtrusive. I lost my fear and got along just fine.

In May, at Open House, I volunteered, the same as I had at the Easter Egg Hunt, to come out on my own time and help. I was learning the hospital more and more. Taking a patient with me, I made trips to most of the buildings. When the dryer in the laundry broke down, we'd go after a bag of wet clothes and take them back, and the three bed wards went together and got the clothes. All morning we were hanging out hospital gowns and taking them in and folding them up. That was in addition to all our other work. We needed gowns.

When we left, I told the afternoon shift about the gowns on the line. She said, "Piss on the gowns." She wasn't going to take any gowns in. So that's the way they felt about it. After we had gone to all that trouble to do what we had, that was the attitude they took. The other shifts were perfectly willing to use the gowns and sheets we had folded, but they wouldn't stoop to fold a gown. I was disgusted. To my surprise, however, when we came to work the next day, the gowns were taken in.

Other times I would take a patient with me and we would go to the laundry and drag big bags full of rags for bathing. The charge would fill three pillow cases full. Two she would leave for the other two shifts, and the third one she would hide for us to have for morning.

I learned where the marking room and the sewing room were and the green house and the drug room. I went through a lot of tunnels, but there were plenty I never saw. I took patients to the beauty parlor and the dentist and special doctors. One patient always insisted that I go in with her when she went to the neurologist, but I wasn't allowed to do that. I would sit in the hall and wait for her.

Sometimes I took them to be staffed, and I would sit outside and wait, wondering all the time what it was like. I would have liked to have observed that. But I was only an attendant.

Toby had gone to Iowa to work on the dairy farm again. Mark was still in the Navy. He was seeing the world on a flight deck. Caroline was working in the college town for the Journalism School. I was still having my problems with my babies and the neighbor kids. When Cynthia and one of the twins got into a fight, it sometimes ended up with their mothers not speaking for awhile, but, after so long a time, it would be smoothed over, and we'd be friends until the next time.

There was one problem, however, that was starting to worry me. Cynthia would be ready for kindergarten in the fall. She would go half a day, but either half would cause problems. I would need to be home.

Now I needed to be on the night shift. We could still take Edward to The House, but there would be Cynthia. I had asked for the 10 to 6 shift when I started, and they refused to give it to me. Would there be any chance of my getting it now?

One day, when the nice supervisor came on the ward, I made a try and asked her if a person could change shifts after they'd been on one.

"Oh, yes," she started to say, and then suddenly, catching the purpose of my question, asked, "Were you thinking of changing?"

"Yes," I answered, "I'd like to get on the night shift."

"No. No." she said, as she threw up her hands and started toward the door. "You can't. When we get a good worker on the morning shift, we don't like to lose her."

She turned back, however, and became more serious, "Yes, you can be changed. Why did you want to be changed?"

I told her the circumstances, and she told me it could be arranged as soon as they found someone to change with me.

I was in no hurry to get changed to the night shift and really didn't expect to be for several weeks at least. This was still the first of July, and it was two months before school started. So on one of my days off, after asking for a transfer, I was completely surprised when Mrs. Best called me and told me I was to be changed immediately, and when I came back to work, I was to report to the night supervisor at 10 o'clock at night instead of 6 a.m.

At the same time, fear shot through me. I would have to get used to new supervisors and would have a complete new set of attendants working with me. I was also used to working the bed wards and knew the patients well. But would they send me to a bed ward? Would they send me to a ward where I had never been before? Would I be all alone?

I was scared, but it was done and I had no choice. I was in a spot and couldn't keep on working if I did not change. Neither the afternoon shift nor the morning shift would fit my schedule.

Chapter 11

Night Shift

I was relieved when I went by the main office, and they told me I was to work on the ambulatory ward across the hall from the first bed ward where I had worked while on days. At least I knew some of the patients over there. I also knew how to get there from the main office. At the same time I had a jittery feeling. The work would be different. All I had been told about the work was that I must make the hourly calls from the ward to make sure we were all right or we weren't sleeping or something.

My worries had been wasted. The attendant on the bed ward was there to meet me at the heavy wire gate into the main hall. She assured me she was charge of both wards. I didn't argue with her. If she said so, I guessed she was. She checked the ward with me and then said, "Take your books and come across the hall with me. We stay over there, and that is where the supervisors pick up the reports." So I took my day book and the daily report and went with her. I was to help her with her work, since there wouldn't be much to do on my ward.

She must have already checked her ward, because we went directly to her office, and she sat down at the desk. I took another chair in the room. She lit her cigarette, and, to my surprise, she placed both feet on the desk and crossed them. Flipping her ashes every so often, she began to talk. I listened, fascinated by her bravery. What if a supervisor or nurse came on the ward? The desk was right in front of the window that faced the day hall where they would enter if they did come. Could she take them down fast enough?

Apparently oblivious of my apprehension, she talked. First, she told me she was charge of both wards, even when the regulars were there. The one on my ward and the other attendant on her ward had been furious, she said, when she was put in charge. She shrugged her shoulders. She didn't care. She began to tell me all the particulars of why. I was a good listener and let her proceed with her monologue.

When she finished with them, she started in on others. She lit in on the regular relief. I had sort of gotten acquainted with the relief and liked her. She was extra friendly and had made it a point to talk to me at the change of shifts. I did know that whenever she had been on the ward that night, the day charge always said with relief, "I know everything is in tip-top shape when she's been here."

From these, she went on to others and warned me who was who and who was untrustworthy. She gave me the low-down on the rules of the game. It was an unforgivable sin to brown-nose and to go from one ward to another and tell anything. It was nobody's business what she did on her ward. I guessed she was giving me fair warning, although it seemed she was taking a keen interest in what was done on other wards. Didn't "what's sauce for the goose is sauce for the gander" hold true here?

At first I hadn't thought too much about it when she settled herself down and talked. I didn't smoke, but I was willing to give the smoker his break. But as the minutes went by and she made the call and still talked on, I began to get fidgety. When did we start work? She talked on. I squirmed with anxiety. What if a supervisor or nurse walks in and catches us not working. She made our hourly call. She was interesting, and in a way she was likable. She certainly had a lot of self-confidence.

At one in the morning, she and I loaded the bath cart with bedpans, sheets and gowns and, with the lights turned on, we went back to the beds. I felt a little more secure. If they came, we would be working.

I wondered why she had placed one of the galvanized pails we had used in the daytime for the bath water on the cart without any water in it. I was shocked when I saw her empty the bedpans in it. I said nothing. It, no doubt, could be cleaned, but it was just the idea. If I were a patient, I would certainly feel funny if I knew the same pail used for my bath had been used to empty bedpans into.

I was also surprised to see her fold up six or seven sheets and place under a few patients, raising their buttocks high in the air. She explained it was against the rules to do this, but it made it easier to change the beds in the morning. All we had to do was to go through the ward and yank the pads from under them, and they would be dry. So that's why we sometimes came on the ward and didn't have a sheet on the shelves at bath time, and we would have to wait until the laundry came in. But then she was boss.

We finished and went back while I got some more low-downs. The supervisor finally came and sat down and visited. It was as if she hadn't really been expecting us to be working. She left, and my partner continued her talking, appearing to be immensely amused.

In the morning, we pulled wet sheets from under the incontinent patients, leaving a dry bed and were done in a short time. I turned on the lights on my ward. Some were slow to get up, but, otherwise, they got up themselves.

The next night, I worked the same ward, but this time the relief attendant was with me. She talked, also, but with her feet on the floor. She gave me some low-downs, but not quite so many. She talked about everything from her family and nursing to the low-downs. She told me about the night-before attendant, and her stories didn't entirely jibe with the other attendant. I had the choice of which one to believe. The two didn't seem to be exactly enemies, but they didn't agree on everything.

I began to worry about being idle the same as I had the night before. But she explained—or tried to—that situation to me. They didn't want us to work on the night shift, she said. She had tried it and had gotten into trouble. A supervisor had caught her scrubbing or something and said to her, "The quickest way to get fired is to work." I could hardly believe it, but since she said it, it must be true, I reasoned. I still felt nervous, waiting for the supervisors to come.

The third night I worked on bed ward A, and it was even worse than ward B. The only time they changed beds was about four in the morning before we went home, and it was actually the worst one, having more incontinent patients than either of the other two. Then I heard their story. The ward doctor, who happened to be the one who had given me the physical when I first came to work, came on the ward one night and caught them with the lights turned on and changing the beds. He was furious, the attendant said, and told them, "I don't ever want to come on this ward again in the middle of the night and catch you waking the patients up."

Well, I supposed it had happened, but I thought it odd that the same rule didn't apply to bed ward C, where I was sent to work the following night. That was his ward, too, and they specialled twice during the night besides the last one in the morning before they went home.

From then on, I went from one bed ward to the another. I seemed to be the bed ward relief. There was one thing they had in common, and that was they used the galvanized pail to empty the bedpans. It bothered me until I finally said something about it to some attendant. They only ignored me.

As the weeks went by, there was something else bothering me. At first, I had felt satisfied and a lot more secure, having worked there for seven months on the day shift. Gradually, as I worked with first one relief and then another who were being sent to wards all over the hospital, they talked about the other wards, and I wondered why I was never sent to those. I would listen to those attendants, some only 19 or 20 years old, tell their stories, indicating they only sent their best attendants to the other wards. One young woman even made the remark about those inferior attendants who could only be sent to bed wards.

I was again feeling the sting of failure. But what I could do? I could only go where the supervisors sent me. I was a no-good attendant. That's what the supervisors thought.

Then there was this thing about being charge. I had been drilled on the morning shift about seniority and signing our names accordingly. I never questioned the rights of the regulars. On the night shift, the new ones were first put through the Infirmary. They usually spent a year more or less in it and then were put out on relief. Most of those who were on relief at the time had a few months seniority on me.

Although the others had from three to five months seniority over me, some of them didn't know one patient from another. If a nurse came and wanted to see a specific patient, I'd have to show her where she was. Still, they said they were charge and wrote up the books and signed their names first. The Infirmary had drilled them in that.

It seemed that it had drilled them in other things, also. Anyone who went through the Infirmary knew it all. I hadn't gone through it. I got the impression I knew nothing, in spite of my having worked on bed wards for seven months on the day shift. Somehow, I almost thought I should know more about a bed ward than they did. But that wasn't the theory. I knew that I knew nothing about the Infirmary.

I continued to feel nervous and jittery just sitting and working jig-saws or reading or just talking, although I realized the supervisors didn't denounce us for not working. On some wards, I would get nervous and go back and fold some gowns or sheets. I knew how hard it was at times to get that work squeezed in on the day shift. I felt it was my duty to help them. I would do this, especially on bed ward A, since it became evident from the first that the charge there was apparently incompetent—no doubt with a very low IQ.

I never tried it on ward B, however, where the attendant who sat with her feet on the desk was charge. But in the mornings, when it was time to special, I would get nervous when she would sit and not start her work (I think she did it deliberately to irritate me) until very late. We usually got done in record time, but I would have my patients to get up afterwards. It would hurry me if we had some trouble. I would get fidgety and go and start loading the bath cart without her starting or taking the lead.

Later, it came to me via the grapevine that she had gone to the office and asked the supervisor, "Is she running that ward, or am I?"

This really made me mad. I had done nothing of the sort. Getting nervous about the cart was the only thing I could think of as anything near that. From then on, however, I never did a thing unless she told me to do it. I waited for the supervisor to come and give me a bawling out, but all she said was, "You must remember those others know more than you do." I felt pretty sure it was this deal she had reference to. It seemed to mean, however, that I was the dumbest person on the night shift.

I felt angry at her, but I had to work with her. We got along fairly well on the surface, and she did have a jolly disposition, always joking and kidding. She amused me. Nevertheless, I wondered what she called her going to the office as if I had done something terribly wrong. She had given me a lecture about brown-nosing that first night I worked with her. If that wasn't brown-nosing, what was it?

As for Josie Armstrong, charge on bed ward A, I was at a loss to know what to do about her. She was proud of her status as charge, and she had been in the hospital a long time and had been charge for years. Yet, she wouldn't get up and start anything unless I moved first, and then she would come trip-tripping behind me. I had to do the starting, or we would never got started. If a patient called from the dormitory or we heard a noise back there, she just sat there until I got up and went.

She had such a happy disposition, too. That bothered me. If I felt angry at her, it was like getting mad at a baby. Occasionally, after listening to her shallow good-natured chattering, I snapped sharply at her and then felt guilty. I felt mean. I knew she couldn't help what she was.

Nevertheless, in spite of those irritations, I was feeling fairly good. When the first of November came, I had been working in the hospital eleven months. I was ready for my first vacation. I took every day, which by including my holidays, took practically the whole month. I enjoyed my vacation, during which time I got a new permanent, a new dress, new shoes and a new outlook on life. I must have been feeling proud of myself.

In fact I was feeling so proud of myself, I had the urge to share it with Dr. Banks. The urge get stronger and stronger. How could I see him? People don't go to see doctors unless they are sick, and I didn't really feel sick. Yet, that urge to see Dr. Banks bugged me. I tried to find something wrong, so as to give me an alibi. After all, I thought, I had been having some trouble. I was being put down a little, although I really liked them, by the reliefs who were belittling me because I hadn't been through the Infirmary.

Finally, I gave in to my urge and called the Baxter County Health Center and got an appointment. Somehow, I didn't relish the idea of coming out to the State Hospital. I might run into someone I knew. I might have a hard time explaining what I was doing there that time of the day.

I also had a hard time explaining to Dr. Banks my reason for coming to see him. He seemed to catch on and said, "Oh, you just wanted to socialize."

I hardly knew how to answer that one, because I had to admit to myself that perhaps he was right. He appeared not to condemn me and talked—socialized, I guessed, it could have been called—about this and that.

I was deeply interested when he told me he was starting group therapy at the State Hospital the next week. He seemed like a sixteen-year old who was getting his driver's license. I took it that it was his first experience with that kind of therapy. I, myself, thought it sounded really fascinating.

I, also, finally got brave enough to tell him about the sock incident. I accused him of doing it deliberately to see how I would respond.

"You thought I would go around wearing unmatched socks all day just for you," he said, unbelieving. "You certainly must be egotistic to think that."

I realized then that he was really right. But why had he done it then? I was puzzled and said, "Was I having hallucinations or something, then?"

"No," he said, "I probably was wearing them accidentally."

It dawned on me that it must have been so. He said it as if it wasn't so out of the ordinary for him to make that kind of mistake. After all, he was human and could have been tired or suffering from a hangover or just daydreaming or thinking. My mistake was in thinking he was more than human.

When it was time for me to go, and he stood up, he suddenly looked down at his feet and then looked at me and smiled sheepishly.

Soon after my vacation was over and I had gone back to work, my problems seemed to be getting worse, or else they bothered me more. Except for a very few times, the supervisors continued to send me only to bed wards. The times I was sent to another ward, there was someone else on an opposite ward who seemed to take over and boss me. I didn't know what it was to be all alone.

On the bed wards, I was being sent to ward A more than any place else. I had to work with Josie more than with anyone else, and she was getting no easier to work with. She was slow, and I was doing much more than my share of the work. She would stand on one side of the bed and hold the patient, while I did any washing or folding of sheets.

Besides being slow, she appeared to get out of work deliberately whenever she could. When one special patient yelled for a bed pan, she would suddenly disappear. It was hard enough to get the patient, who wouldn't help herself at all, on the bed pan when there were two of us, but for one, it was a backbreaking job. I usually had the job to do alone. She never took a temperature, and one day, thinking that she might not know how, I tried to teach her. I spent 15 minutes and finally gave it up as hopeless. Someone told me, "She's smarter than you are. She knows that if she doesn't know how, she doesn't have to do it."

But what should I do? If I didn't take it, it wouldn't be taken. One night after my two days off, I came to work and noticed that the temperature hadn't been taken on a patient who was running a very high one the first night, but the second night it had been charted. As Josie and I sat, she began talking about taking the temperature. She kept referring to it as though she had taken it herself. I wondered about it and asked her, and she told me she had.

The next night, I was working with the attendant who had worked with her the past two nights. She was upholding Josie mostly, I thought, because when she worked with her, she could do as she pleased. "Did Josie take that temperature?" I asked the attendant, who happened to be a general relief over the whole hospital.

"No," she said, "I noticed she didn't do it the first night, so I thought she didn't know how, and I offered to do it for her the next night."

I told her what Josie had told me, and she was furious. So, I thought, she was getting a taste of what Josie could do. I'd had Josie sit and tell me things that I absolutely knew weren't the truth, but she did it so innocently, I almost believed her. She was certainly clever in some ways. I had to hand it to her.

Nevertheless, I got disgusted with myself whenever I snapped angrily at her. I felt mean like when I had snapped at Phil's mother. Josie was always so happy and never seemed to notice when I got irritable. She had a way of getting out of work and giving the excuse she was charge. She would leave the ward ten minutes before six in order to catch the bus, saying she had a right to since she was charge. She had to catch the first bus, she'd say, oblivious of the fact that I had small children at home and she had none.

As time went on, I was getting more and more disgusted with the Merit System. It was unfair. Since Josie had been there so much longer, she got $44 a month more money than I did. It looked fair to her and to a lot of others. The Merit System was the thing. I couldn't see it. There is no way, regardless of where a person works, that the work and wages can be divided equally. But where could a person doing one-third of the work get a lot more money than the one doing the two-thirds? The grading system was unrealistic. The grades were based on the supervisor's or nurse's personal opinion and how many run-ins the attendant had with them.

One supervisor might give an attendant a high grade, while another one might give the same attendant a low grade. Unless the grade would be the same no matter who did the grading, it couldn't be fair. Anyone taking a test in arithmetic or spelling with 100 problems or words and missing five would always get the same grade of 95, no matter who did the grading. The grading needs to be less subjective and more objective.

Besides, how could any supervisor or nurse, no matter how smart, grade an attendant on the 100% basis, when they'd worked eight hours a day for about 240 days a year? Sometimes, I'd tell Josie how I felt about the Merit System, but it would slide off her back. She thought she deserved more money than I got.

There was one purpose for the Merit System, I thought, and that was to keep the union from getting a toe-hold. The System gave the worker a certain amount of protection after the first six months, and it played that up. But the truth was that the higher-ups made all the rules, and the workers had no voice in making them at all. The little man could only take what was dished out to him. But the union was weak, and there was nothing I could do except rave now and then.

Everybody, except maybe for the first six months for beginners' pay, should get the same, unless the raises came automatically at intervals spaced realistically until they reached the top and didn't depend on whether a supervisor liked the attendant or whether the state had any money. The state could get the money if they wanted to. Some get raises with regularity, and others don't.

In spite of my getting less money, I still tried to do my work. Mrs. Wheeler, the morning charge, began to notice a difference in the ward when I was on and told me several times that she wished they'd put me in charge. Although I didn't do it on other wards or on this one if somebody besides Josie was taking charge, I folded gowns and such.

I wasn't so enthusiastic about the idea of being in charge, however, since I had on the other ward across the hall, where the attendants changed beds three times instead of once. The two regulars were farm women, and it seemed we had more in common. I would have liked to be regular relief on it. But then, I had little hope to get it. It never entered my mind to ask for it. I was sure if I did, they would give me anything else but that.

I didn't work with Josie all the time, however. The relief would take charge, except for one exception who would have nothing to do with the books and made me take care of them. She seldom worked the bed wards and thought she shouldn't be charge, in spite of seniority. The others, however, insisted on being charge, and I didn't argue with them.

But that didn't bother me as much as the others bragging about where they were sent. They made me feel so insignificant. One night I was working with a relief when she started telling me about when she had been on the morning shift. She had worked in the intensive treatment building, she said, and had helped give ECT. Just talking about it made me feel nervous. She was touching a sensitive spot in me.

But when she started telling me how the doctor had turned it over to her and let her give it by herself, I found myself feeling more than the normal anxiety. She was trying to show her superiority over me. She had given shock treatments, and I hadn't even seen one given, which really hadn't been a strong desire of mine. Taking them was enough. I didn't want to see one given.

Still, I began to feel a little angry at her. In the first, place, I couldn't imagine a doctor doing such a thing as turning that over to an attendant. I told her she hadn't given it. I didn't believe it. She might have helped in the room, but no doctor would let an attendant do that. She insisted he did. He even left the room while she gave it, she said.

Mingled with a feeling of inferiority because of her professed importance was a rising anger because of what I felt was definitely an exaggeration, if not an untruth. I was seeing red. I lashed out at her, "Listen, I've had shock treatments, and if I ever hear that my doctor turned it over to anyone who knew no more than an attendant, I'm going to give him a piece of my mind."

She was taken aback by that and never said any more about having given the treatments. We talked about other things, but the next night she worked with me again, and she brought it up and admitted she hadn't actually given the treatments. The doctor had let her trip the lever, or whatever it was, but he had the thing set and stayed in the room all the time.

Nevertheless, I still felt inferior when the others talked about all the other wards they were sent to. I knew very little about anything except that one building and then mostly just the bed wards. The ones who had gone through the Infirmary still talked like if you didn't go through it, you didn't know anything. So one night I asked the supervisor to let me go over there and work some night so I could see what it was like. She promised me she would.

She did one night. The other three women over there all had less seniority, and one had only been working a week. They made sure I signed my name on the bottom. I didn't really care, since I knew that I knew nothing about the work there. But wasn't it the same principal, when those coming out of the Infirmary who had never worked a bed ward automatically took charge? She sent me there a second night, and that was it.

I also asked her to send me to the receiving ward in the intensive treatment building. That was another ward that was being held up to me as so important. They only sent their best attendants over there, I was told. The supervisor tried to make some excuses why she couldn't send me there. They had to have someone with experience, she said. But since there were always two on that ward, I wondered why they couldn't send me with one of those. How did the others get experience? Anyway, she never got around to sending me there.

So I kept right on working bed wards, while I listened to the glowing tales about the other more important wards where the good attendants went. I knew I wasn't alone, however, because there were the few who were regulars on these wards, so that was some consolation.

One night, I was working with a relief who had worked the bed wards more than most of the relief attendants. She had a jig-saw puzzle on a table in the day hall, and we were working it. I heard a call from the dormitory for a drink of water. I started to get up, but the other woman said, "Don't get her one. It'll just spoil her."

I sat back down, remembering the raking over the coals I had gotten about the patients being dehydrated. I also remembered the supervisor telling me I must remember these others all knew more than I did.

I was still feeling some of the rejection I had felt at first. I know I'd gotten in trouble for folding sheets and such. If I did it, they'd all have to do it. They didn't want me folding gowns on Josie's ward either.

But one thing that had bothered me from the first was to sit and listen to the night attendants gripe about the day attendants and how they never did any work. I knew better and had tried to defend the day shift. But it occurred to me that I was only alienating my fellow workers. I kept still. Nevertheless, I still felt the rejection.

In some ways I felt better when I worked with Josie, but after several nights, she'd get on my nerves. A few hours might be all right, but eight hours two or three nights a week was almost too much for me. I'd be so tired sometimes when I went home and hated myself for getting cranky with her occasionally.

Finally, I began to feel I couldn't stand the work any longer. I wanted to quit my job. I again had an urge to see Dr. Banks— this time really feeling a need. But what could he do? I didn't know. I just wanted to see him. I wanted my crutch. So I called the Health Center and got an appointment.

When I went to see him, driving about 60 miles (although he came to this city once a week, and I could have seen him just as easily by driving across the city), he seemed to be on another one of his sarcastic binges. He didn't act very sympathetic. He could understand my getting bored with Josie, all right, he said, but why didn't I tell her to shut up and go someplace else and sit. He didn't understand this hospital. I would be an outcast for sure, I thought, if I high-hatted her and sat by myself. Besides, telling her to shut up would only make me feel more guilty than ever. I already felt mean enough.

Then he said, when he learned I'd been working mostly on bed wards, "What business do they have keeping you on a bed ward?" Then he added, "It's all right to work them some; it gives you humility, but you shouldn't stay on them."

I didn't tell him why I thought they sent me on a bed ward—because I was one of the no-good attendants. I guessed I didn't want to let him know I was that much of a failure.

When I left, he said, "You don't have to drive this far to see me. Next time, get an appointment at the State Hospital."

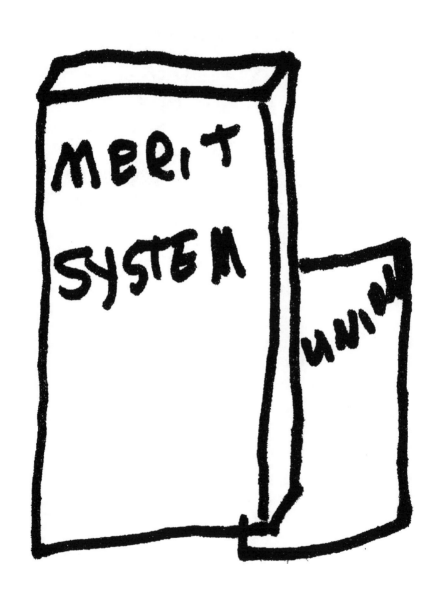

Chapter 12

Coping with Jealous Co-workers

We had a new superintendent, and he was making a lot of new changes. He had hired a director of nursing, who was doing a bang-up job of changing things, too. Nobody seemed to know when she slept, because she would pop in on the wards any time of the night, and I supposed it was the same way in the daytime. Her assistant seemed a little more human, maybe.

In all this turmoil, they were starting a new system of education. The first course offered was one called Interpersonal Relationship, and anyone could go who wished. No promotion or wage increase was promised for this, and we had to go on our own time. I decided to go. The director of nursing's assistant taught the class I was in. It was a large group and consisted of attendants and supervisors and one person who didn't even work in the hospital.

It was in the afternoon, so I rode the bus out there and back. I became acquainted with attendants on other shifts, giving me a little lift in spirits.

The course consisted of lectures, demonstrations, tests and just a general confusion of arguments at times. I usually took some part in it, even though my fear of speaking up just about got me. I got good grades on the tests, but a young afternoon attendant got better than I did. She seemed to take a liking to me and I to her, in spite of our seeming so much different. She certainly would have pleased Dr. Banks, I thought. Her grooming was perfect. Anyway, we seemed to become friends, and we got better acquainted on the bus.

I also got acquainted with Mrs. Oliver, another afternoon attendant. She rode the bus also. I had met her at some union meetings and thought she was extra nice. I sort of forgot about my feelings of rejection at work and had a good time.

One day, our teacher was giving a lecture on ECT and suddenly asked why bobby pins and other metal things were taken off the patient before a treatment.

Without thinking, I held up my hand and said, "to keep from making burn marks on the patient."

"See," the nurse said, sounding as if she'd discovered a new thing. "If attendants can feel that way, how do you expect patients to feel?"

I suddenly felt guilty. That was exactly how I had felt when I had taken them.

It really was an interesting course, and I enjoyed it, and after we finished, we all got a little card giving us credit for so many hours. That was our diploma.

After several classes of this course, classes for psychiatric aides would be started. These were the first, and there was no guarantee when they would get promoted with a pay raise. It would probably come sometime. Only attendant II's could take it, so that left me out. Only HA II's who were already promoted had to take it, but those who had taken their test and passed, but hadn't yet been appointed, could take it but they didn't have to. So this left me out of the first class. The hospital administration was anxious to get the hospital accredited, so this class was going to be crash course—short and sweet. They wanted some PA's in a hurry.

I was back to the some old grind. I was relief and taking my orders from most of the other reliefs as well as the regulars and writing my name at the bottom of the list while I listened to the tales of the other wards.

One night I was listening to an attendant tell about the intensive treatment building and, especially, the receiving ward. She said that it was different from the other buildings. The patients' charts over there were more complete, and she could read everything.

That wasn't all she was telling me. It wasn't just the patients' charts who were currently there that she could read. There was a room where the charts of every patient who was in the hospital at the time and every patient who had ever been in the hospital were kept. She could get into the room and read any chart she wanted to. This sort of surprised me, since I had thought the old charts were kept in the administration building. But maybe it was true. If it weren't, why did she say it was?

But that wasn't what was worrying me. A sudden fear hit me. Whether all the charts were there or not wasn't important. I felt pretty sure my chart was in that building. That's where Dr. Banks had talked to me, and I knew he had my chart there then. It might still be there. Could these other attendants get their hands on my chart?

A kind of an anger took hold of me. These other attendants were so smart and knew everything, it seemed, but this was something different. They had no right to read my chart. Even though I felt at times the other attendants told me these things because they knew I was green, and it made them feel big to tell somebody who knew nothing. I was hurt.

I kept still and let her talk, but when I went home, I called the social worker at the State Hospital and got another appointment with Dr. Banks. This time I felt I had a legitimate reason for seeing him. He couldn't say I was asking for sympathy.

When I told him why I had come, he soon set my mind at ease. "No one except Mrs. Bird (the social worker) has access to your chart. Not even your superintendent can get his hands on it. But if it will make you feel any better, I'll have Mrs. Bird get it, and I'll take it with me to my office."

I told him it would, and I saw Mrs. Bird bring it to him. I went home feeling a little like I had out-smarted these smart attendants.

One morning Josie and I were finishing our last patient and were hurrying. It was almost time to go home. Suddenly we heard a loud noise in the utility room. Leaving the patient we were working on, we rushed outside. There on the utility room floor was one of our little senile patients. She was a pest, hiding behind doors and, when we went by, stepping out and whamming us one or something. This time she must have climbed into the utility sink where we washed our bed pans and used it as a stool because there was a large BM in it. She had evidently fallen off the thing which was about 30 inches from the floor.

We carried her to her bed and finished our other patient and Josie made a dash for the door to meet her bus. I was left, as usual, to finish up the work. Mrs. Wheeler came and I tried to explain to her what had happened.

"Did Josie make out an incident report?" she asked.

"No," I told her.

She was angry and said, "I'm getting tired of making out someone else's incident reports."

"I'll make it out," I said.

"No," she said, "it's not your place. She's charge, and she should have made it out. I'll just wait and not make it out, and if one needs to be made out, I'll make her make it out when she comes back."

That night, I was working on the ward across the hall when early in the night the supervisor and the nurse came on the ward madder than a couple of prize-fighting roosters. We hadn't made out an incident report, and it turned out the patient had a broken hip.

All I could say was that I wasn't charge and thought I wasn't supposed to make it out. They gave me to understand I was just as responsible as if I were charge.

This had me confounded. Once the supervisor had told me I was to remember that the others all knew more than I did. I was to do what the others told me to do. Now she was placing the responsibility onto me. That's what they had been doing all the time. They left Josie as charge, but expected the others to take the lead. I had noticed they were careful who worked with her. I was one of them—one who would put up with her. I wondered how she had ever passed the test and then learned she had come before they had to take the test.

Later in the night, the supervisor returned and informed me I was being placed on the ward with Josie as a regular, but I was to be charge. They were moving the other attendant, so we were to be the regulars on the ward. I was stunned, but what was there to do except obey.

Nevertheless, I wasn't prepared for my reception the next night when I came to work. In the hall I met one attendant, and she just turned her head and never spoke I went cold all over. The story had gotten around that I'd been put in charge. But why the cold shoulder? What had I done? The truth was, I knew, she was blaming me. For what? Because Josie had been taken off charge?

Then I remembered who the attendant was. It was Mrs. Gilbert. She'd been put in charge of bed ward B when the attendant who sat with her feet on the desk had been moved. I had worked with Mrs. Gilbert a few times and knew how she could talk about anyone she disliked. I had never been sure how she felt about me, although she had acted friendly enough. Now I knew regardless of how she'd felt before, she was down on me now. What she thought wasn't important, I decided.

But when I met another attendant in the hall who had been extra friendly to me and had even brought me a mess of fish she caught, and she also turned her head and didn't speak, I knew I was in for it. Still, I knew this attendant as a sort of notionate individual, and although I felt a stab of pain, I thought perhaps it wasn't too important either. How would others feel about it?

Although most of the others spoke, I was sure I detected a note of coldness in their voices. Now I was scared. What had I done? The supervisor and nurse had done it. Did everybody hate me? What could I do? I must go to work, and I was charge. I could make some of the rules now. Do I dare? I had no intention of turning the ward upside down, but I had some ideas.

But Mrs. Wheeler, the morning charge, had wanted me to put one pad under four or five patients who usually voided more than the average. She told me by the time they were able to get back to the beds after giving breakfast, these patients were swimming. Just one pad to soak up the moisture was all she asked me to put on the bed, and these only on those few patients. I could certainly sympathize with her and thought the request was reasonable. I tried to please.

But Mrs. Adams didn't see it that way. The office said we weren't supposed to pad the beds. I wasn't doing what our night supervisors said for us to do. She made a sarcastic remark. I was tense and scared. The thought struck me that I must hold my own. The supervisors were catching us both, I thought. Could I give orders, and could she take them. She was under scrutiny, as well as I was. It was as much for her sake as mine, I reasoned, that I mustn't let her win.

Later in the night, while making a bed, I got a catch in my back. It just came and left and didn't bother me too much that night, but when I went home, it started bothering me. I remembered what had happened during the night. I would have to work with her that night. I wished that there was some way to keep from going to work that night.

I thought and thought and thought about it, until, one night, when the supervisor came on the ward, I asked to speak to her alone. I told her about the pail incident, and she said, "If it bothers you, you have a right to change that. You are charge."

I also asked her about the padding, and she said, "We want to get along with the other shifts, if possible. Do what she wants you to do, if it will help the day shift."

So that was it; I had my orders from my night supervisor. I was in the clear so far. I worked a few more nights with Josie. She was her happy self, but when I saw her sitting and signing her name below mine, I could tell it hurt her a lot. She had been so proud of that honor.

I suddenly felt sorry for her. What was the difference who signed her name first. After all, she did have seniority over me—a lot of it. She'd been doing it all these years. Why should she stop now? It simply wasn't that important. So, in a fit of sympathy, I let her sign her name above mine. She seemed happy.

Nevertheless, she still seemed a little reluctant to special three times and didn't like the bed pan deal. One night, she said, "I heard you went to the supervisors and asked them to put you in charge."

Stunned, I asked, "Who told you that?"

"I'm not going to tell you," she said, sounding a little defiant.

"You don't believe it, do you?" I asked.

"Yes, I do," she said, still sounding like she had something on me.

"But you know that if I had asked them to do that, it would have been the last thing they would have done."

She still insisted she believed she had been taken off charge simply because I had asked the supervisors to put me in charge. I couldn't be sure why they'd done it, but I could guess. Making the change the night after the incident report thing should have been one indication. Besides, I was sure some of the higher-ups were beginning to see her as she was. If it hadn't been me, it would have been somebody else.

At the time, I had seemed to be the most logical one. I had been working with her for some time. They knew that not everybody would have worked with her. I, myself, had heard some make just that very remark—that they'd refuse even to work with Josie. But here I was, trying desperately to defend myself. I hadn't asked for it and, in fact, hadn't wished it.

I tried some more to pry out of her who had told her that. I, somehow, believed someone really had told her, and she hadn't made it up. She flatly refused, wanting to believe it, I thought. I gave up and said, "You don't have to tell me. I know who said it." I told her I was pretty sure it was Mrs. Gilbert. She didn't deny it. I had sat for hours and listened to her tear to pieces others whom she disliked. Her actions in the hall were certainly an indication. But at the same time, I knew there was no way to stop it. I'd have to live with it. It didn't look easy to me. Anyway, Josie was friendly, even if she did think those things.

Then the day came for me to work with Mrs. Adams again. While we were back specialling in the morning, and when I said we were to put pads under some patients, she snapped, angrily, "Whose orders are you following—the morning shift or our night supervisor?"

"Our night supervisor," I told her coldly. "I asked her about it, and she said for me to do what the day shift wanted me to do as long as it is reasonable. She wants us to get along with the other shifts."

Nevertheless, I was anxious. She acted as if she might defy me and refuse to do what I said. What could I do? She was on the verge of telling me to go to hell.

Later, I had a catch in my back. It didn't last long, but it did surprise me. Although Amelia had always had a lot of trouble with her back, mine had never given me much trouble. I always thought back trouble was a psychosomatic disease, but at the time I hadn't let it enter my mind that this was my problem now. It was only a catch and wouldn't amount to anything.

But when I went home, it got worse. After sleeping, it hurt when I started to get up. Phil came home, and it continued to hurt. I expected to go to work, even though I was extremely distressed. How would I handle Mrs. Adams? Suppose she flatly refused to do what I told her to do. I hadn't been throwing orders around. I hadn't even asked her to go back and fold gowns. I watered the patients in the morning myself, and let my helper do as she pleased.

Besides, my reception in the hall was getting no better. Several turned their heads, and the others were a question. I felt the coldness. I had no backing. If only I didn't have to go to work. But there was no way out. I must go.

My back got worse and worse. Finally, I tried to walk to the kitchen and couldn't make it until I got Phil's mother's crutches and used them. I was thinking about taking a sick day.

But I wasn't really sick. It was just my back. I had such a good record. I had worked a year and a half before even taking one day, and that had been for Edward and Cynthia, when they had been in the hospital. Edward had come down with pneumonia, and Cynthia had a bad cold. Then I had planned to go to work, until I took one look at Edward's face as I was getting ready to leave him and go to work.

But to take a sick day for myself seemed unthinkable. I couldn't take a sick day. Phil insisted I stay home. Finally, I said, "If they would let me work on some ward other than a bed ward tonight, I might be able to do the work."

Phil said with authority, "If you're not able to work your regular ward, you're not able to work at all. You're staying home."

I stayed home.

The next day my back continued to hurt. It was getting no better. During the day I continued to think about what to do that night—go to work or stay at home. I remembered how I had seen others have back trouble and had believed it was psychosomatic. I had never questioned that their pain was real, but I was sure it had started in their minds.

Gradually, a light began to shine. What was my problem now except psychosomatic? It got clearer and clearer. I was dreading to go to work. I was entirely conscious of that fact. Yet, I felt guilty about staying home because of that. In fact, it wasn't a legitimate excuse. I couldn't tell the supervisors that I was staying home because I dreaded facing one attendant and the rejection I knew would greet me. I knew I must face it. My "super-ego" was at work.

But, subconsciously, my "id" was at work. It had no conscience. Save yourself, it was saying. But my conscience said differently. Well, my "id" was saying, I'll fix that for you. I'll give you a real reason for staying home. And this was it. My backache was real. It had started entirely on the subconscious level.

Suddenly, I felt angry at my subconscious. It had no right to do this to me. Almost miraculously, but not so surprisingly to me, my backache began to get better. It improved so much that when it was time to go to work, I was well. What, I wondered, would some of these people who denied the power of the subconscious say to this? No doubt, I thought, they would say it was ready to get better. How could I prove it?

Anyway, I had whipped that ogre in my subconscious for the time being, at least. I still had my problem of facing the turned heads and cold greetings and working with attendants who plainly hated me. I felt terrible. The pain in my chest seemed unbearable. I felt like a worm. I wasn't eating worms; I was the worm. I couldn't stand this, I thought. I went to the supervisor and asked her to take me off as charge. She told me this usually happened in cases like this. She put me in charge because that's where she wanted me. I'd had nothing to do with it, she assured me.

"Try it awhile longer," she said, "and if it gets too tough for you, come and tell me, and I'll take you off."

So there was nothing for me to do, except go on as I had. I still felt like an outcast, but as I looked around, I saw one or two attendants who I felt might be on my side. It helped some, but the general feeling of rejection continued. When I worked with some new attendant I had never seen before, and she would give me a cold shoulder, I knew what was behind it. Mrs. Gilbert's stories were doing their damage. Everyone had my number about what a cad—or rat or whatever—I was before they ever saw me. I had no way to combat it. It was her word against mine.

July and August went by. Two months had passed since I'd been put in charge. The first psychiatric aide class was about to finish. I had no hope of going to the next one that would start in September. I was sure I didn't have enough seniority. But I had gone to that interpersonal relationship course and had learned that, in spite of my age, I could still study and take tests; although I now found I forgot things so much more easily than when I was younger. I remembered Dr. Banks' telling me I should go to college, and a sudden desire to go came over me. Yet, I didn't really think I could go, even when I made the remark to someone that I was thinking about it.

September came. Chuck was a senior, and Henry was now a freshman. Cynthia was in the First grade, and Edward had started kindergarten. I now had a time when I could sleep without kids to watch. Henry, however, still carried papers, and if he missed a paper or a dog got it and he had already left for school, I would have to take it. In the beginning, I'd had to drag the two babies with me or leave them and run to carry the paper to an angry customer who wanted the paper right now. I'd run home, not sure what I'd find at home. Henry was an extra good paper boy, but even the best made mistakes at times.

I was surprised, however, when the supervisor told me I was to go to the next PA class. I wasn't sure why but thought it might have been because I had said something about going to school on my own. Maybe it had made them think I was a willing recruit. Then I thought it might be because I was charge of a bed ward. Whatever it was, it was another thing for my enemies to talk about. Yet, there were others who went with less seniority than I had. I had no idea why I was picked to go.

After so long, I thought I knew. I heard remarks all around me about how others felt about the school. "Nobody would get me to go to the school." "We'll never get anything out of it." "Unless they promise us something, I wouldn't go." It seemed that anyone who went was a fool. I decided the head office might have had a hard time getting anyone interested. They took the willing ones. So many just sneered at the idea. Yet, it gave room for my enemies to say that I was a pet and had been brown-nosing.

But who were the ones guilty of that, I wondered. I learned that Mrs. Adams had gone to the office and had complained about me, but I also heard that she'd been told to go back and do what I told her to do. I was boss. I would call her going to office brown-nosing.

Again, we had to come out to class in the daytime on our own time. We went three hours from 1:00 p.m. to 4:00 p.m. two days a week, and we'd go for seven months. I enjoyed the classes, although I got terribly bored at times, studying about the bones, the heart, the muscles, and all that sort of thing. We had a little about the mental end of it, but even it wasn't new. I felt more interest in it, but I had read so much about psychology that I would get tired of listening to the nurse get up and repeat it all.

But to remember the names of the bones and the muscles and the ventricles and the glands, I found, wasn't exactly easy. I'd think I knew them and two hours later, I couldn't remember whether the tibia was a bone in the arm or the leg, and the muscles were worse. I was getting old, or else it was the shock treatments still working on me.

Nevertheless, I made a pretty good showing on the little tests we had every few days, even though the ages of the students ranged from the 18 or 19-year-olds to those even older than I was. My friend on the afternoon shift who always had everything about her in perfect order again got about the highest grades. We were still friends.

In spite of my enjoyment, I was feeling more and more tired. I still had to work with Josie, and, although I was over her, I would get terribly irritated with her at times and would feel guilty about it. She still got $44 more money than I got. I saw some good in her, too. I'd see her stoop down and love some little lady curled up in the fetal position with pain written on her face, and the little lady would get a contented look on her face. Many of the so-called good attendants would never have done that. Love was the answer. That was the big thing to some of these who never saw a relative or friend. Even Josie had something to give.

Nevertheless, trying to get everything to make sense to me was getting me down. I was hated, and it wasn't just some paranoid ideas, either. I could feel it all around me. Little things came back to me. I had treated Josie so mean by taking her job away from her. She and the attendant whom they had moved to make it easy for me had been making it so well until I came along and upset everything by brown-nosing. Yet, I knew I had not gone to the office on her, in spite of everything. I hadn't gone to the office on anyone, but they had gone to the office on me.

I seemed to get lower and lower and really didn't know what was wrong with me. I don't know why I did what I did. I knew he couldn't do anything for me. I just felt an urge to see him, as if he might give me a new lease on life. I was boss, but at the same time I was a failure. I couldn't stand it, I thought. I called the social worker and made an appointment with Dr. Banks. I was again reaching for my crutch.

He reacted the way I'd been afraid he might and had hoped he wouldn't. He sat and listened with what I thought was no show of understanding. I was boss, so what was my problem? Really, I didn't know. I had trouble explaining the situation to him, and I wasn't sure he was getting the picture. He told me he thought I was the best attendant in the hospital, but even that didn't help. How could the best attendant in the hospital be so hated?

I went home feeling a little like my trip had been wasted. He simply didn't see the true situation.

Chapter 13

Working the Men's Ward

It was November, 1961. I'd been working at the state hospital for two years, and I was ready to take my second vacation. I needed a rest, not just from Josie, but also from the rejection, which was worse. I had never gone back to the supervisors to ask them to take me off as charge. I was still toughing it out. I had found a few who had no feeling of friendship for Mrs. Gilbert and who let her stories roll off their backs. Yet, I was still trying to find a way to get away from it.

In the meantime, along with these PA classes, there was talk of placing women on men's wards, which so far hadn't been done. There was a ward in the basement of the intensive treatment building I hadn't known existed. I guessed it was going to be one of the pioneer wards for women, and it seemed they were asking for volunteers.

Immediately, there was a general uproar about how terrible it would be to put women on male wards. I heard all around me the remarks from women saying they would never work a men's ward.

I was a little bit lost, trying to understand this attitude. Nurses and aides in other hospitals cared for both women and men, but some said their husband wouldn't let them. Others seemed to think that there was only one thing bound to happen if women were working with men. I made the remark that I would be willing to work on a men's ward if they asked me. I doubted, however, they'd ever ask me.

I heard one attendant say she'd work the ward if they'd move the colored man who was a regular on the ward. I thought right then that leaves her out. I was sure they wouldn't do that for any woman. Women weren't that important to the ward. I said, "I don't care what color he is, just as long as he treats me all right."

I was still terribly surprised when, just before my vacation, the supervisor came to me and said they were putting me on that ward as soon as I came back from my vacation, which would be about the whole month.

Along with the surprise came a fear. What had I done? Had the supervisors gotten wind that I had said I would work on a men's ward. Maybe the other women were correct in being reluctant about it. But it was done now. I had never refused to go anywhere I had been asked to go.

All I knew about why they had moved me was that the supervisor said when she told me about it, "You've done such a good job cleaning this ward up, we're sending you over there to clean it up." I really didn't know for certain what she meant by that, but imagined the men might not be keeping the ward too clean. But then, I had about a month to sleep on that.

During my vacation, Chuck had a birthday, and at the ripe old age of 17, he decided to enlist in the Marine Reserves while still in high school. He would have to go someplace for training on the weekends. He had been in the ROTC for his third year and had been in the Honor Guard and was pretty good in shooting ability and had gone places for contests and such. This was different, however. But when he insisted, Phil relented and signed up for him since he was underage.

When I went back to work after my vacation, I was expecting to go right on the male ward. After several days of my not being told to go over there, I started believing they had changed their minds. At the time, they had put a woman on the ward temporarily, but she had given them to understand that's all she would work it. She would work until they found someone else.

The attendant they had sent over there was going to the same PA class I was, so I got a chance to hear what she had to say about it. It needed cleaning, all right, she said, but she was going to refuse to stay on the ward. The patients were mostly ambulatory, but were older men. I still felt a little nervous and waited for them to tell me to go. But as the month of December passed and no one notified me, I was beginning to think they had decided to keep the other woman after all, in spite of what she said. I was almost feeling glad.

But when the first of January came, a supervisor came to the ward and told me I was to go over to the male ward. She assured me I would never be alone on the ward with the patients; there would always be a man attendant with me.

There was something, however, that bothered me. I was being told I was to clean things up, but, no doubt, the men would be in charge of the ward. No one had told me any differently. What should I do? Was I to take orders from the men? Suppose they didn't tell me to clean and scrub. The supervisor had told me in the beginning I must remember the others knew more than I did. Should I wait for the men to tell me to clean?

So to make sure, I asked her, "Should I go ahead and work or scrub without the men telling me to do it, or do I have to do just what they tell me to do?"

"You can do any cleaning you want to do without anyone telling you to do it. Nothing will be said," she assured me. So that was that; I had my orders.

I made my way through the tunnel with a bend in it so one couldn't see the end and with the huge pipes carrying the steam heat from one building to another. The heat was terrific, and the roar gave me the feeling the pipes would explode at any minute. At the end of the tunnel, I found myself in the basement of the building where I had consulted Dr. Banks. I followed the supervisor's directions and came to the door at the far end.

Timorously, I put my key in the door and opened it. The inside of the ward was made on the same order all the wards in the newer buildings were, with a large day hall and at the other end the office with a window making it possible for the attendant to see what was going on in the room. A hallway, with rooms on both sides, led back to the dormitory where most of the patients slept in one large room.

It was different, however, in that the windows were high above the heads of anyone who might be in the room, with a ledge reaching to the small windows. I saw the office before me with a couple of men in it. At the time, I was vaguely aware of one more difference between it and all the women's wards where I had been. Gum wrappers, cigarette butts, ashes and scraps of paper littered the floor.

In fact, I wasn't interested in those things at the moment; I was thinking about the two men in the office. I had never met either one. I walked toward them, wondering what kind of reception I might receive. After all, this was sort of an insult to them—to have a woman come on the ward to clean it up. Yet, I guessed that was what lots of men thought women were for—to clean up after them.

Both men greeted me respectfully and then let me sign my name under theirs. I learned later that I had seniority over them both, but that didn't worry me. I had expected that they would be over me. After we signed, I wasn't sure what to do. But when Joe, the colored man, who must have been in his early thirties, got a broom and pails out and started scrubbing the patients' stool room out, I helped him. He also scrubbed the hallway.

Mr. Sherman, who was supposed to be charge, did some of the other work while we scrubbed. I thought, they scrub after all. But when we finished the hall and the stool room, Joe seemed to be done. Now I wasn't sure what to do. Should I wait for them to do some more cleaning? The day room certainly needed something, so I got the broom when I saw the men had no intention of doing any more cleaning.

I swept the gum wrappers and cigarette butts and ashes off the floor. It looked a lot better, but it wasn't clean. I wasn't sure what to do now. In spite of what the supervisor had told me, I was afraid to go any further. Would the men think I was taking too much on myself. I still couldn't forget the attendant going to the office and asking if she was running the ward or was I.

Mr. Sherman sat down in the office at the desk. Joe got his college text book and started to study. I had my psychiatric lessons to get, so I started to study them. I'll have plenty of time, I thought, to do any cleaning later on. I had seen the dried-on BM on the floor and on about a third of the new aluminum-handled chairs, but to go on out there and start scrubbing might be pushing things too far. I was between two fires. Should I wait for the men to tell what to do or do it on my own?

Later in the night, I got up enough nerve to get a pan of water and wash off the chairs. That's all I did. In the morning, I did what the men told me to do to help the old men find their chair or fasten their suspenders or put on their shoes.

The following night, while Joe scrubbed out the stool room and the hallway, I swept the day hall and then got a mop and pail and started scrubbing the floor. Mr. Sherman came and helped me move the chairs to the center of the room and then got a mop and helped me. I took no extra pains that night. The chairs, again, had BM on them, and I cleaned them off later.

The next night, I worked alone with Mr. Sherman. He did Joe's job and let me do the scrubbing alone, but he did help me move the chairs. I noticed the spit on the floor was much harder to get off than the BM. I must get me a putty knife, flashed through my mind.

From then on, I worked some nights with both Joe and Mr. Sherman and other nights alone with either Joe or the older man. Other nights, I worked with one or the other and one of the young college boys. They had been given the night shift deliberately so they would have time to study. At least that was the way I had heard it.

Anyway, after the first few nights, no matter who worked with me, I had no help. I let the men take care of the stool room and the hallway, and I did the rest. I got me a putty knife, and while they sat in the office and did the book work or did nothing, I scraped spit off the gray cement floor. Every night I washed the chairs, about a third of them having dried-on BM. I learned one man—he wasn't such an old man either—wouldn't leave his overalls on and would go from one chair to another. I had the feeling he knew perfectly well what he was doing and did it deliberately to irritate the attendants.

It didn't bother me, however, that I had the scrubbing to do alone. I could do it anytime I wished and would spell it off with studying my PA lessons. Joe and the younger college boys studied, too, but Mr. Sherman didn't read or sleep, which, of course, he wasn't supposed to do, or do anything except to sit and stare into space. He was friendly, but he didn't talk either.

Joe was different, though. He had his college textbooks and would find some controversial question and get me involved in it. He seemed to love a good argument, although he would get so wrapped up in it and so rambunctious, I had a hard time getting in my side.

One night, one of the young boys told him to shut up and give me a chance to tell my side of it. Then one night, we were discussing a religious question and I mentioned the two trees spoken of in the Garden of Eden.

"There were no two trees in the Garden of Eden," he said.

"There was," I said. "There was the Tree of Life and the Tree of Knowledge of Good and Evil."

But he insisted he was right, and finally to prove it to him, I started to hunt for a Bible. I said I knew there had to be one on the ward. There had to be a Gideon Bible, I thought. I turned everything upside down hunting for it and finally located one in a small room on a shelf at the bottom of a stack of books.

He still insisted. Even in black and white, I couldn't seem to convince him. But the next night, he brought it up himself and said, "You were right. There were two trees."

Later, the young boy working with us said to me, "You know, that's the first time I ever heard him admit he was wrong."

Nevertheless, he seemed to enjoy himself. In fact, shortly after I had started working on that ward, he said, "It's a lot more interesting with you here. Mr. Sherman never talks all night long, and it gets tiresome."

I also thought it was more interesting to talk to him than it had been to visit with Josie, who only read True Story magazines, if she read anything. I also had a chance to talk to some of the patients in the middle of the night. Here, if the patient was quiet and wanted to sit in the day hall, he did. On the women's wards, the first thing the supervisors expected you to do if a patient got up was to shoo her off to bed or get an order for some medicine to make her sleep.

Mr. Sherman and Joe paid no attention to the patients, but when a patient appeared to want to talk, I talked to him. One very depressed man would get up at night and seemed to enjoy having someone to talk to him. He claimed he had ulcers, and he wanted something to eat. I had spells with my stomach that I diagnosed myself as ulcers or something bordering on that and knew how milk could help it.

So I asked the men if they cared if I warmed some milk for him and gave him some crackers. They wouldn't bother with it, they said, but if I wanted to do it, it was all right with them.

Except for his depression, the man seemed well in contact with reality, and when one little senile patient who was kept in a side room would come out into the hall without a stitch of clothes on, the depressed man would point his finger at him and say, "Get back in that room; there's a lady on the ward."

That wasn't supposed to make any difference, I thought. When I agreed to work on this ward, I should have been ready to expect anything. Yet, there did seem to be a different attitude of the men toward me than toward the male attendants. Mr. Sherman noticed it and said, "I think it is good for these men to have a woman on the ward. They seem more contented or something."

I thought about this when one little bachelor who had lived with his unmarried sister all his life would come up to me and thrust out his arm with his long-sleeved blue chambray shirt. A button was missing from the sleeve, and he would call me by his sister's name and ask me to sew on the button. He never asked the men to do it.

I also noticed that some men would get a broom and try to help me. They seemed to be more careful about their cigarettes and ashes and gum wrappers. It dawned on me that most of these men had been raised by mothers who had waited on them, then later by sisters and wives. Now they were thrown into an all male world. They had been used to being dependent on women. I could see where just having a woman on the ward could help them, whether the woman did any scrubbing or not.

I was really feeling fairly well satisfied on this ward. I decided I liked it better than the women's wards. When Mr. Sherman was working, everything went along smoothly. He worked quietly with the men, and I helped him with anything he asked me to do—mostly helping the men with their shoes or socks or to find a chair in the day hall and even sometimes to help them to put on their overalls.

Except for one small man, who seemed to think he was at his best and would try to grab me and kiss me, I had no trouble with any of the men. Since he took steps about three inches long and would have had trouble catching up with a snail, I didn't have any trouble with him; I stayed an arm's length away from him. If I'd had the face and figure of a movie star, it might have been different. Since I didn't have, those problems were nonexistent.

Later, when there was a shortage of workers on the women's wards, I was moved back to the women's wards. For a few weeks I was on relief and would sometimes be sent to work one of the bed wards. But mostly now I relieved on the women's wards in the building that was so terribly important that I had been hearing so much about. I even relieved on the women's receiving ward a time or two. Then one day I was surprised to be told I was to be regular relief on the ward that was considered the most important ward in the hospital, where all those attendants said they only sent their best attendants.

In some ways, I felt a little disappointed in leaving the men's ward. I had actually liked it better than the women's wards. Now here I was, ready to start working the ward that just a few months before I had thought was the most unattainable ward in the Hospital.

Chapter 14

Conclusion

This isn't the end of the story. There's a lot more—group therapy, more experiences working at the State Hospital, ups and downs of raising the children to adulthood, arrival of grandchildren—but this is as far as I will go in this volume. As you recall, this started out as an assignment by my psychiatrist to write seven pages of the first seven years of my life. I hated that assignment, as I had always hated writing assignments, but I suppose it was therapeutic. It helped me to put my feelings into words, and it helped the doctor to get a background on what my problems were. I also found that the more I wrote, the easier it became. Obviously, I got over that initial writer's block. I ended up with thirty-six chapters, nine hundred typewritten pages and a word count of about 230,000. As I progressed in the writing, it changed from being an autobiography to a mission to expose shock treatments as a barbaric practice that should join the ranks of other long-abandoned and ineffective treatments for the mentally ill. I feel as if they robbed me of part of my mind—sort of a lobotomy without the knife. I don't think they helped me at all. I think that talking out my problems with someone who would listen was the most effective. In addition to my opinions concerning shock treatments, you will have found in this book my opinions about many other things concerning the treatment of the mentally ill. I hope that this will be helpful to those who have been on either side of the fence—either as a patient or as a caregiver.

Epilogue

Notes from Her Children and Grandchildren

Caroline:

Reading this manuscript was a real eye-opener for me. There are things that I wish I had realized when I was a self-centered ungrateful teenager. I had no idea that she was hurting as much as she was. One thing really struck me: I find it incredible that my mother was ever considered weak and nervous. She was one of the strongest and most stable persons I have ever known. I think her detractors didn't really understand her. I question the competence of some of the professionals who attempted to treat her. I don't think any of the psychiatrists had any clue as to what she was handling in her day-to-day life in the face of numerous adversities.

A lesser person would have caved under the load of responsibilities that she was shouldering quite bravely. On the farm, we didn't have indoor plumbing or central heat, and electricity came when I was in grade school. After Dad went to work in the city, Mom had the farm to take care of without any modern machinery or any decent outbuildings. The barns burned down when I was very young, and they were never rebuilt.

One thing I do fault her with is that she seemed to find it easier to do things herself than to teach us kids to do them. We could have been a lot more help if she had expected more from us. She faithfully got up before daybreak every morning and built the fire and made breakfast and got us kids up to get ready to go to school. And we weren't easy kids to wake up; it was a struggle every morning. She could have thrown up her hands and said, "Be that way. Sleep your life away. See if I care," but she didn't. There were mornings when we were in the country school that she would kill a chicken and dress it and fry it so we would have something good to take to school in our lunches. She taught us a lot that could be considered enrichment in addition to what we were learning at school. She instilled in us a love of reading. We were poor, but one thing we had in our home was books. When I was in the fourth grade, she taught Mark how to extract square root (No, not on a hand held calculator; this was 1950.), and he went to school and taught the rest of us how to do it. How many other parents could have done that?

In the book, she mentions that Dr. Banks said that *unfortunately* she had a high IQ. That sounds strange, but a high IQ can be a liability. It reminds me of a radio drama I heard back in the days when radio was more than music, news and talk. It was a science fiction show, and I think the title was something like "The Land of the Blind." It was a story about a man who woke up and found himself in a strange land peopled by beings that were just like human beings except that one facial feature was totally absent. They had no eyes. As often happens in science fiction stories, everybody speaks English. He kept referring to seeing things and talking about colors and light and dark. They decided that he was insane and that the only way to cure him was to operate and remove those two unnecessary features on his face. In some ways, a high IQ—especially in a woman—is regarded the same way the sightless beings in that story regarded eyes.

She expressed many times that her purpose for writing the book was to remove shock treatment from psychiatry's repertoire of treatment for the mentally ill. Maybe the shock treatments helped her, but I doubt it. It did mess with her memory for a while, at least, but she treasured her memory. It was what enabled her to excel academically. Her doctor said at one point that her problem was that she remembered too much. It wasn't so much that she remembered too much as it was that she held those memories in her psyche and agonized over them more than the average person would have. She was extremely conscientious and was always concerned with doing the right thing. She took responsibilities to heart and couldn't let go of her sense of responsibility in any situation that confronted her.

She may have put more blame on the shock treatments than they deserved. The short-term memory loss certainly was there, but when you read the book and see the details that she recounts, you have difficulty believing that there was a serious long-term memory loss. As for the increasing difficulty with remembering people's names, I have found as I have reached the age she was when she was writing the book, that is a common but disconcerting natural part of the aging process. In talking with my friends, I find it happens to all of us. And I used to be so good with names. Another thing I have found to be so annoying the last few years is when words that once had been such a common part of my vocabulary suddenly become so elusive. (No, I didn't have to go to the thesaurus to find "elusive," but I might have to tomorrow. I'm getting to where I almost have to carry a thesaurus with me.)

It is abundantly clear that she suffered from social anxiety. How much of that was an inborn genetic trait and how much from the fact that she grew up in a remote rural area of Montana with few social contacts outside of her immediate family we will never know. Maybe some people thought she was antisocial or a snob. It always bothered her that everyone in our neighborhood called each other by their first names, but everyone called her Mrs. Eastman. We kids could never come up with an answer to her as to why that was. Now we see commercials on television all the time for prescription pills to treat social anxiety, and I suspect there are people who see those commercials and cajole their doctors into prescribing those pills simply to make themselves braver in social situations. Mom would have been a more apt candidate for that medication if it had been available then.

I also wonder if some of the physical manifestations that she describes could have been symptoms of a pre-diabetic condition. Both of her parents were type II diabetics, and she was diagnosed with type II diabetes in later adulthood. I know from my own personal experience that type II diabetes can manifest itself in various ways decades before one starts showing any elevated blood sugar level. I wonder if the stiffened finger syndrome that she describes could have been hypoglycemic episodes resulting from the insulin resistance trait, which is what ultimately leads to the pancreatic malfunctions which lead to the diagnosis of diabetes. The medical profession seems to be a little slow in putting that all together, along with the connection between a woman's menstrual cycle and migraine headaches and the ingestion of simple sugar at the wrong time in the cycle—many years before the diagnosis of diabetes.

In view of things that have come to light since our parents have passed on and some of the things in this book, I think perhaps Dad was more in need of psychiatric help than Mom was, but no one would have ever believed it at the time. He was so outgoing and gregarious and made friends so easily, everyone loved him. Whenever we went to town and he left us in the car so he could run into the store to get something, it always took longer than it should to get that one item. We always said, "Daddy found someone to talk to." But he would never have believed that he needed help. After all, life seemed to be going along fine for him; what was the problem?

The author and her husband with their 7 children at the younger daughter's wedding

Karen Steltenpohl (Granddaughter):

On behalf of my sister and me, our years with Grandma found her to be a pillar of strength, unconditional love, and most of all, sheer joy. Her image still planted in my mind could be comical to some, as she was a farm woman unconcerned with fashion or latest hairdos. She mostly dressed in homemade clothing ; our favorite was the house dress, otherwise known as a moo moo to most. Her remaining five teeth or maybe just three were clearly visible as she burst into her infectious laugh that cackled like a rooster crow. She wore those hose with the garter belt. I always thought it was fun to fasten them for her, regardless, she still got the elephant legs by mid-afternoon when we were shopping downtown. Her car was a red station wagon with the whole back filled with water jugs in case of an over-heated engine, which didn't happen much, as she mostly was a putt-putt kind of driver. But there were the occasions she stepped on the gas and threw our heads back against the seat with our hair flying wildly. We liked those rides a little more. Old Red could only turn right, because she hated crossing traffic, until the cops got her leaving the laundromat. A simple lady she was, but quite complex in her inner soul.

At Grandma's house we composed and performed our piano concerts, Twinkle Twinkle Little Star known to most, on the out-of-tune old piano in the front bedroom. She believed in us, so we believed it too. We made stuff on the sewing machine, played work and wrote books like her on the old typewriter with sticky keys, learned to crochet, planted flowers, and collected green stamps to win stuff at the Safeway store. She got a bird so we could teach it to talk, but it didn't catch on, so she bought a bunch of birds for her to talk to. Her dog was Buttons, a shaggy black and white pooch with an endless smile and by her side to the end. It was at her house I created the Fluffer-Nutter sandwich, marshmallow Fluff and peanut butter, and ate Vienna sausages from the can. We could just always be anything we wanted to be, and she took the time to be with us when Dad was asleep from the night shift and step-monster, his wife, was acting a beast. She never spoke out, but I think she always knew her house was our retreat.

As a pregnant teen she did not judge, and as I ate green olives like mad she shared that she had done the same with my dad. She taught us about Montana, her Swedish roots, and meeting Grandpa. The farm was her life, and I remember when she worked nights but would always wake up for us to visit. She managed her children, grown or not; their troubles were hers, especially waking uncle up to get to his job. The house was a big two-storey filled to the brim, but all for a cause. Papers were waiting for the cub scouts to collect for a paper drive, cans rinsed out and reused to start plants from seed or transplant some houseplant starts. Jars had a purpose, furniture in case someone needed a spare, fabric and yarn for all her projects not yet complete. Books galore floor to ceiling in the living room, but a passion she passed on to both of us. If a question came up, she would pull out a book, and we would study the subject together, even though I'm now sure she already knew the answer. Her stuff was all for a purpose, as previously stated, but one of two times she let me have it was when I threw away a glass jar, so I know better than all why not to do that ever again. How was I to know that cattle could cut their feet when the trash got carried off to the ditch, but I was informed and then it was over; lesson learned.

I remember Grandpa in his death bed with her always checking on him, placing his favorite lemon cookies at bedside even though he hardly ate, and never did I feel he was that bad; she comforted us just right. She looked after neighbors when they fell ill or their kids had moved away. She loved all the kids who would play in the yard. For a short while before my wedding my son and I moved in with Grandma, and she was thrilled to have him around. It often carried her back to stories from my childhood. She said she always said I was a thinker as she could see in my eyes the wheels turning. I now think she may have seen herself a little bit as she was that very way, and most times with so many thoughts turning, she would get scattered. Grandma told everyone I would finish her book one day, and it is with great honor that I'm doing that in a round-about way.

Finally, there was the second time she told me what she thought, and that was when I was marrying a Catholic. It was a firm conversation with her belief clearly spoken. However, she was front row that day in the church. A few weeks later she was suddenly taken. My sister had last seen her a short time before she called uncle to get her to the hospital. I made it just after she passed, but I held her hand and told her goodbye one final time. We were distraught, and as I had to select her dress from the closet and take it to the funeral home with tears flooding my view of the road, I vowed to myself to just always do the right thing the way she had shown me. My sister and I still hold her dear and speak of her often with a certain peace that we got to be individuals with dreams and belief in ourselves without regard for what others thought because Grandma loves us. Her sister at the graveside weeping in hysterics on her knees obviously had also known her strength, love, and joy way before us.

Emily Baumann (granddaughter):

I never got the chance to know my grandmother; she passed away before I was born, and because of this, I have always felt a void in my life. I often would ask my parents to tell me stories growing up about my grandma, and they always obliged. These stories only made me feel deeper sadness at a young age when I came to understand what passing on really meant. No, I really wouldn't get a chance to ever hug, share stories, or eat a family dinner with her. This is a hard lesson for a young child to try to learn. How do you process a loss, when you didn't even know what was missing?

A few years after my birth it came to light that she had written a book, and in that book she gave herself an alias: Emily. How strange that she had given herself the same name as her future granddaughter, a granddaughter that she would never know. When my parents told me about this, I was maybe ten years old at the time, and I instantly felt that connection that I had been missing all those years. Here it was in these meticulously hand-typed pages of a massive book, in which she gave herself my name. Names have power, and this shared name has given me the ability to truly grieve the loss of a grandmother and also connect with her from beyond the veil.

I remember my father spending countless late nights slowly hand-scanning the pages of his mother's book into the computer and carefully fixing the mistakes when technology would throw a wrench into things. Bless him for his fortitude and dedication to digitizing this manuscript for our family to share. He would read excerpts to me from her book as he scanned, and my connection with my grandmother grew stronger through her words.

Several years ago she appeared to me (just once) in a vision. In that vision, she directed me to get her book published to share her message and story with the world. She was very certain that the world needed to hear these things and that her book was not meant to sit in a box. I am so excited to share her words and her wish to publish. As a granddaughter that never knew her, I grow closer to her with every word, and I hope as the reader you do to.

I have come to realize that the spirits of our passed loved ones, and especially those who we never knew, live on within us every day. For me I have this book, the stories my family has shared, and the power of the uncanny coincidence of our shared name, Emily.

Christina Branson (granddaughter):

My grandmother was already an old woman when I came along. We shared an affinity for jigsaw puzzles and photography, and she got me started (much to my father's dismay) keeping parakeets, but I never really got to know her well. It wasn't until my mother gave me the full manuscript of her mother's memoirs that I began to learn how much we had in common. My now-ex-husband, with his freshly minted creative writing degree, deemed the work unpublishable, but I continued to make a study of it, learning not only about her but in the process learning much about myself.

Some things I learned too late to save myself from shared struggles, and some revelations have me marveling at the lucky twists of fate that spared me other painful episodes. Every time I delve into the world of my grandmother's memories, I find something new to ponder, something new to explore within myself. Some of you reading this will not, of course, be as closely connected to her, but I hope all the same that you have found some valuable insights in her story.

Author (holding grandchild) and her husband and several of
their grandchildren

The author on her wedding day June 26th 1938

Printed in the United States
By Bookmasters